500

indian dishes

500

indian dishes

the only compendium of indian dishes you'll ever need

Meena Agarwal

APPLE

A Quintet Book

First published in the UK in 2013 by
Apple Press
7 Greenland Street
London NW1 0ND
United Kingdom

www.apple-press.com

ISBN: 978 1 84543 478 6
QTT.FHIN

This book was conceived, designed, and produced by
Quintet Publishing Limited
6 Blundell Street
London N7 9BH
United Kingdom

Food Stylist: Fern Green
Photographer: Ian Garlick
Art Director: Michael Charles
Editorial Director: Donna Gregory
Publisher: Mark Searle

10 9 8 7 6 5 4 3 2 1

Printed in China by 1010 Printing International Ltd.

All images in the book © Quintet Publishing, unless otherwise stated.
© Shutterstock: p. 27, 50; © Stockfood: p. 130.

contents

introduction

India is as diverse in its food as it is in its people. If you were to start from the very north and move slowly southwards, stopping in every state, province and major city, you would taste an incredible variety of food along the way. A simple meal of lentils or dal, which is one of the main staples in an Indian diet, has as many variations to it as the number of homes that cook them.

For many Indian families, Saturday nights are spent entertaining, amid mighty quantities of succulent foods – Indians love to shower people with their hospitality and delight in sharing meals with them. Food holds a very special place in any Indian household, and no festivity is complete without a table laden with colourful dishes end to end, enough to please a king. It's no wonder that out of all the rooms in their homes, many Indians take the most pride in showing you their kitchens.

Food is not just something enjoyed in the home, however. Anyone who has ever walked the streets of a major Indian city, be it Delhi, Mumbai or Bangalore, will attest to the fact that no evening stroll is complete without making a stop at one of the many street vendors' stalls that surround every busy area. Street after street, stall after stall, you will be greeted by tempting plates that urge you to give them a try. Smothered with spicy and tangy chutneys, yogurt and other fixings, each dish is a different adventure.

This book will help you recreate the wonderful variety of flavours and textures in Indian cooking, using equipment and ingredients that are easily accessible outside India. From tempting pakodas to hearty curries and mouth-watering sides, you will be amazed at how quick and easy it can be to create a whole new world of flavour in your own kitchen.

Home-style Chicken Curry, page 88

Most Indian food relies on a small selection of key spices

ingredients

The majority of the ingredients used in Indian cooking are easy to find outside India. A few may be a little harder to come by, but if you don't have a local Indian shop, you can often make subsitutions using other ingredients.

spices

If you've never cooked Indian food before, and the only spice in your kitchen is curry powder, don't fret: begin with the basics. These five key spices will help you cook many delicious Indian meals without having to splurge on an endless proliferation of exotic flavours:

cumin: Mainly found in north Indian food, cumin is often used for its strong, distinctive taste: a mildly sweet, smoky flavour. It can be used as whole seeds or in powder form.

coriander: One of the most commonly used spices in Indian cooking, coriander lends a mild, soothing aroma to curries, and is often added to enhance more robust flavours. Used in powder form.

turmeric: This spice is mainly used in Indian cooking for the gorgeous yellow colour it gives to dishes, and for its medicinal properties. Turmeric is widely used throughout Asia to treat stomach and liver ailments, and externally to heal sores and bruises. Used in powder form.

red chilli powder: Indian red chilli powder is made from ground dried red chillies; it is much hotter than the standard chilli powders available in many western nations.

Lentils are flavourful additions to your Indian menu

garam masala: This aromatic spice blend includes a variety of spices, including cumin, fennel, coriander, cardamom, cinnamon, cloves, pepper and red chilli. It is mostly added towards the end of the cooking process, so that its full aroma is not lost. Almost every Indian home has its own secret recipe for garam masala.

Once you have these staple spices and are confident about using them, try out amchur powder, chaat masala, curry leaves, kasoori methi and sambhar powder. Each of these spices has a very distinct flavour and will elevate your cooking to a whole new level.

lentils

Lentils come in varied sizes, shapes and colours, and each variety has its own distinct flavour and recommended cooking time. They do not require much of an effort as far as cooking is concerned, and yet you can have variety in your meals simply by alternating the kinds of lentils you use. Some of the most common lentils are:

masoor dal (red lentils): Red split masoor lentils are the most commonly used in Indian homes. They take the shortest time to cook and require no pre-soaking whatsoever. This type of lentils is usually found in everyday meals and can form the base of a quick dish when you're running short of time.

toor or arhar dal (yellow lentils): Toor lentils are dull yellow in colour and are often used as the base for south Indian specialties such as Sambhar. They need to soak for a few hours before cooking, and take longer to boil down to a soft, edible centre. A quick way to overcome the long cooking process is to use a pressure cooker. They also cook perfectly in a slow cooker.

chana dal (split-pea lentils): Chana dal, or split-pea lentils, have a deep yellow colour and look like the halves of a chickpea, only in a smaller size. They take the longest time to cook and are suitable for the pressure cooker and the slow cooker. They are often used for special dishes and are a favourite to serve at dinner parties.

moong dal (green lentils): These lentils are set apart from the others listed above by their green colour and bean shape. They are rarely used in preparing everyday meals, but are the star of a widely loved dessert called Moong Dal Halwa. In the West they are sometimes called mung beans.

other ingredients

chickpea flour (besan): Also known as gram flour, cici flour, chana flour and garbanzo bean flour, this is a fine flour made of ground chickpeas. If necessary you can substitute plain flour, but the flavour will not be the same.

cooking oil: Many Indian dishes are cooked using oil. You can use your preferred oil, but it is a good idea to use a light oil, such as corn or rapeseed oil. In India many of these dishes would be cooked using ghee, a clarified butter, but using a light oil is considerably healthier.

instant dosa flour: A dosa is a pancake made from rice flour and ground pulses. The ingredients for this are all included in instant dosa flour – just add water.

paneer: This is a soft Indian cheese that is used in many dishes. It is a perfect substitute for meat when making vegetarian curries. If you can't find paneer you can use firm tofu instead.

Paneer Butter Masala, page 166

tamarind: This fruit lends a distinctive flavour to many Indian dishes, and forms the basis of a wonderful chutney (see page 269).

yoghurt: This is a common ingredient in Indian dishes, and forms the basis of many marinades. It tenderises meat and gives dishes a distinctive flavour. You can use any natural full fat or low fat yoghurt in these dishes.

desserts

Although a decent Indian meal can easily be replicated by people trying their hand at it for the first time, traditional Indian desserts are in a class of their own. The majority are milk-based and work well when made in huge quantities. Often, however, they are not the easiest things to prepare, taking a lot more time than many people would usually be willing to spend on a sweet treat. Even in India, traditional Indian sweets are rarely made at home; they are most often bought from sellers that specialise in them.

If you'd like to create a dinner menu complete with a treat after the big meal, Indian shops in major cities will often sell Indian sweets, many of them elaborately decorated and packaged. Try *barfi*, delicately flavoured desserts made of condensed milk and often decorated with silver leaf, or *jalebi*, coils of batter fried and drenched in syrup, or any of a multitude of others.

It's also easy to take a popular dessert choice and make it Indian-inspired. Try, for instance, rice pudding with cardamom and cashews or raisins thrown in. Or a fruit salad with a saffron-infused syrup or coconut milk. Another wonderfully exotic treat to serve at any gathering is a platterful of dark chocolate truffles, infused with chilli and cardamom powder and rolled over crushed almonds.

Fruit salad with coconut milk, a tasty Indian-inspired dessert

appetisers

Indian cuisine is full of delicious, flavourful dishes
that work perfectly as appetisers. Try these tempting
treats whenever you have friends or family over,
and watch them clean their plates with delight.

fish cutlets

see variations page 45

These cutlets are a much healthier way to enjoy the goodness of fishcakes; they don't need the addition of cream or mayonnaise to be delicious.

2 medium boneless fillets of firm white fish
   (about 450 g/1 lb)
1 large potato, boiled and mashed
2 tbsp onion, finely chopped
2 tbsp fresh coriander leaves, finely chopped
2 tbsp fresh lemon juice

2 tbsp breadcrumbs
$1/2$ tsp red chilli powder
$1/4$ tsp turmeric powder
$1/2$ tsp cumin powder
salt, to taste
light cooking oil for frying

Chop up the fish into tiny pieces. Mix and mash together all the other ingredients, except oil, in a bowl to blend well. Divide into eight parts, and form each part into a cutlet.

Heat 2–3 tablespoons of oil in a large non-stick frying pan. Shallow-fry the fish cutlets until brown and crisp on both sides, adding more oil if necessary. Fry in batches to avoid overcrowding the pan.

Serves 4

masala meatballs

see variations page 46

On busy weekdays, I like to turn these meatballs into large burger-sized patties and serve them between toasted buns with salad and chutney on the side.

450 g (1 lb) ground chicken
1 beaten egg
$1/2$ tsp red chilli powder
$1/2$ tsp garam masala
$1/2$ tsp chopped ginger

$1/2$ tsp chopped garlic
2 tbsp breadcrumbs
salt, to taste
light cooking oil for frying

Mix all the ingredients, except the oil, in a bowl. Form into bite-sized balls and fry in a little oil until meatballs are brown on all sides and cooked through. Drain on kitchen towel to soak up excess oil, and serve warm.

Serves 6

gobi manchurian

see variations page 47

This is a highly popular dish in India, which can be found on many street corners throughout the country. Street vendors make them fresh to order, and watching them being cooked in front your eyes is as much of a delight as eating them is. *Gobi* means cauliflower.

60 g (2 oz) white rice flour
60 g (2 oz) cornflour
$^1/_4$ tsp red chilli powder
$^1/_4$ tsp garlic powder or 1 tsp minced
    fresh garlic
120 ml (4 fl oz) water
1 medium-sized cauliflower, broken into
    bite-sized florets
light cooking oil for deep frying
1 tbsp ginger, finely chopped
1 tbsp garlic, finely chopped
1 tbsp green chilli, including seeds,
    finely chopped

1 medium-sized onion,
    finely chopped
$^1/_4$ tsp ground white pepper
salt to taste
2 tbsp soy sauce
2 tbsp chilli–garlic sauce
2 tbsp ketchup
60 ml (2 fl oz) water
fresh coriander leaves, finely chopped,
    for garnish
spring onion, finely chopped,
    for garnish

In a bowl, combine rice flour, cornflour, red chilli powder, garlic and some water (about 60 ml/2 fl oz) and mix with a fork to form a batter thick enough to coat each cauliflower floret. Heat enough oil in a deep frying pan to deep-fry. Coat each floret well by dipping it in batter and deep-fry until golden brown and crisp. Strain excess oil from the frying pan and set oil and cauliflower aside.

Heat 2 tablespoons of the reserved oil in a large wok. Add the chopped ginger, chopped garlic and green chilli, and sauté for a few seconds until fragrant. Add in chopped onions, white pepper and salt, and fry for few minutes until onions soften.

Add soy sauce, chilli–garlic sauce and ketchup; mix well. Add in water and let the sauce come to a boil so that it starts to thicken.

Add the cauliflower florets and stir fry to coat well with the sauce. Garnish with chopped spring onions and coriander.

Serves 6

spicy potato wedges

see variations page 48

These Indian-inspired potatoes make a great change from rice as an accompaniment for curries, and also pair perfectly with roasted chicken or lamb.

6 medium-sized potatoes, skins on, cut
   into wedges (about 8 per potato)
2 tbsp light cooking oil
$^{1}/_{2}$ tsp red chilli powder
$^{1}/_{2}$ tsp coriander powder

$^{1}/_{2}$ tsp cumin powder
$^{1}/_{4}$ tsp garam masala
$^{1}/_{4}$ tsp amchur powder
salt, to taste

Preheat oven to 200°C/Gas Mark 6 (400°F).

Put all the ingredients onto a large baking tray and mix thoroughly so that each potato wedge is well coated with the blend of spices.

Arrange potatoes in a single layer on the baking tray and bake for 20–25 minutes, turning them over once after 10 minutes, until potatoes are cooked through and crisp.

Serves 6

coriander paneer pakodas

see variations page 49

These are bound to disappear fast, so make sure you save yourself a piece or two before handing them out. Some people call them *pakoras*.

85 g (3 oz) fresh coriander leaves, chopped
1 clove of garlic
1 green chilli, including seeds
salt, pinch
water, as needed
225 g (8 oz) of paneer, cut into 5-cm (2-in) slices, 1 cm ($^1/_2$ inch) thick

120 g (4 oz) chickpea flour (besan)
$^1/_4$ tsp red chilli powder
$^1/_4$ tsp amchur powder
1 tsp fennel seeds
salt, to taste
2 tbsp water
light cooking oil for deep frying

Put coriander, garlic, green chilli, a pinch of salt and some water in a blender and blend to a thick, smooth paste.

Spread a thin layer of the coriander paste between 2 slices of paneer to make a sandwich and set aside. Do this for all the squares of paneer.

In a bowl, mix a smooth batter with chickpea flour, red chilli powder, amchur, fennel seeds, salt and water, almost like the consistency of thick pancake batter. Dip each paneer sandwich into the batter to coat well, and deep-fry until golden and crisp. Drain pakodas on kitchen towels and serve.

Serves 4

samosas

see variations page 50

For a quick dinner option, serve these traditional vegetarian samosas with rice and a large side salad.

400 g (14 oz) plain flour
1 tsp salt
2 tbsp light cooking oil
water, as needed
2 tbsp light cooking oil
1 tsp cumin seeds
1 tsp coriander seeds
1 small onion, finely chopped
$^1/_2$ tsp red chilli powder
$^1/_4$ tsp turmeric powder

1 tsp coriander powder
$^1/_2$ tsp garam masala
salt, to taste
3 medium-sized potatoes, boiled and
    chopped into tiny cubes
85 g (3 oz) frozen peas, thawed
2 tbsp fresh coriander leaves, finely
    chopped, plus extra to garnish
oil for deep frying

Mix the flour with salt and oil, and knead with water to form a smooth, soft dough. Divide the dough into golf-ball-sized balls, cover with a damp towel and set aside for 15–20 minutes.

Heat oil in a large wok, and sauté cumin and coriander seeds until they start to sizzle. Add in onion and fry until it softens.

Stir in chilli powder, turmeric, coriander, garam masala and salt, and sauté for a few seconds. Add in potatoes and peas, and mix well to combine. Let mixture cook for a few minutes to allow the flavours to blend, stirring occasionally. Add in fresh coriander, and mix well again. Set aside to cool to room temperature.

Roll out the dough balls into circular discs about 0.5-cm (¼-in) thick, and cut each circle in half. Taking one semi-circle, roll from one end to the other forming a cone. Press the edge of the cone slightly with your fingers to prevent it from opening.

Fill the cone with the potato and pea mixture. Press edges together to tightly close, forming a pyramid-like shape. Do the same for the remaining dough balls. Deep fry samosas in hot oil until golden and crisp on all sides. Serve garnished with coriander.

Serves 6

fish pakodas

see variations page 51

When choosing a fish for this recipe, opt for one that has a subtle and mild flavour, to prevent it from overpowering the overall taste of the batter.

260 g (9 oz) chickpea flour (besan)
$^1/_4$ tsp red chilli powder
$^1/_4$ tsp amchur powder
$^1/_2$ tsp garam masala
1 tsp fennel seeds
salt, to taste

water, as needed
light cooking oil for deep-frying
3 medium-sized firm white fish fillets
    (about 450 g/1 lb total), cut into
    2.5-cm (1-in) thick pieces

Using all the ingredients except fish and oil, mix a smooth, pancake-like batter in a bowl.

Heat oil in a deep pan. Dip each piece of fish into the batter to coat well, and deep-fry until golden and crisp. Drain fish on kitchen towel to remove excess oil.

Serves 6

paneer tikka pizza

see variations page 52

This is a perfect example of how fusion cooking can give you the best of both worlds.

260 g (9 oz) paneer block, cut into tiny cubes
1/2 tsp red chilli powder
1/2 tsp coriander powder
1/2 tsp cumin powder
1/4 tsp amchur powder
salt, to taste
1 tbsp light cooking oil
1 tbsp fresh lemon juice
1 large ready-made pizza crust, unfrozen

85 g (3 oz) cup pizza sauce
1 small onion, thinly sliced
1/2 green pepper, thinly sliced,
    without seeds
1 jalapeño pepper, thinly sliced,
    including seeds
140 g (5 oz) grated mozzarella cheese
2 tbsp fresh coriander leaves,
    finely chopped

Marinate paneer with the spices, salt, oil and lemon juice, and set aside for 15–20 minutes.

Preheat oven to 175°C/Gas Mark 4 (350°F). To assemble the pizza, spread the sauce evenly over the pizza base. Top with onions, green peppers, jalapeño and marinated paneer, making sure that all the toppings are spread out evenly. Sprinkle mozzarella cheese on top.

Bake in the oven for 15–20 minutes, or until cheese starts to bubble. Garnish with fresh coriander leaves and serve.

Serves 4

masala chicken wings

see variations page 53

The next time you're in the mood to order in some hot wings, try this version instead. The blend of spices is just enough to tickle your taste buds without setting them on fire.

12 chicken wings, skin on
$\frac{1}{2}$ tsp red chilli powder
$\frac{1}{2}$ tsp coriander powder
$\frac{1}{2}$ tsp cumin powder
$\frac{1}{2}$ tsp garam masala
$\frac{1}{4}$ tsp amchur powder

1 tbsp garlic paste
1 tbsp ginger paste
1 tbsp tomato paste
2 tbsp fresh lemon juice
2 tbsp light cooking oil
salt and pepper, to taste

Mix all the ingredients in a bowl, making sure that each wing is well coated with spices. Set aside to marinate for a minimum of 30 minutes in the fridge.

Preheat oven to 200°C/Gas Mark 6 (400°F). Spread the chicken wings evenly on a foil-lined baking tray, so that they do not touch. Bake for 15–20 minutes, flipping once, until chicken is cooked through and starts to crisp up.

Serves 4

paneer croquettes

see variations page 54

This Indian take on an American classic is a good way to introduce kids to different flavours by experimenting with their long-time favourites.

260 g (9 oz) paneer, grated
2 large potatoes, boiled and mashed
$^1/_4$ tsp red chilli powder
$^1/_2$ tsp coriander powder
$^1/_2$ tsp cumin powder

$^1/_2$ tsp garlic powder
salt and pepper, to taste
2 eggs, beaten
225 g (8 oz) breadcrumbs
light cooking oil, as needed

In a bowl, mix paneer, potatoes, spices, garlic, salt and pepper to blend well.

Heat enough oil for deep-frying in a deep frying pan. Form the mixture into golf-ball-sized balls and roll each ball between the palms of your hands to form a cylinder. Dip each croquette into beaten egg, and then roll it in breadcrumbs to coat well on all sides.

Deep-fry the croquettes until golden and crisp. Drain on kitchen towel and serve warm.

Serves 6

curried carrot soup

see variations page 55

This is perfect soup to warm up with on a chilly or rainy night. Serve with naans or chapatis for a perfect quick meal.

1 tbsp light cooking oil
1 small onion, finely chopped
2 garlic cloves, minced
4 large carrots, peeled and steamed
$^1/_4$ tsp turmeric
$^1/_2$ tsp red chilli powder

$^1/_2$ tsp coriander powder
$^1/_4$ tsp cumin powder
1 tsp dried parsley flakes
about 1 l (34 fl oz) chicken or vegetable stock
salt and pepper, to taste

Heat oil in a deep pan and sauté onion and garlic for a few minutes until tender. Roughly chop up steamed carrots and add them to the pan, along with the turmeric, chilli, coriander and cumin powders and dried parsley flakes. Sauté for a few minutes, until the carrots are coated well with the spices and start to caramelise around their sides.

Add in the chicken or vegetable stock, let it come to the boil, and allow to simmer for 10–15 minutes. Season with salt and pepper, and allow the soup to cool.

Once the soup has come to room temperature, puree it in the blender. Heat through once more and serve warm. If the soup becomes too thick, add in a little more broth or water, and allow it to come to the boil again.

Serves 4

cucumber & yoghurt soup

see variations page 56

This soup is a wonderful addition to a light summer lunch. Serve it chilled in shot glasses for a fun treat.

400 g (12 oz) natural yoghurt, full fat or low fat
240 ml (8 fl oz) water
1/4 tsp red chilli powder
1/4 tsp cumin powder
1 tsp minced garlic

2 tbsp fresh coriander leaves, chopped
1 tbsp lemon juice
260 g (9 oz) grated cucumber
salt, to taste

Put yoghurt, water, chilli powder, cumin powder, garlic, coriander leaves and lemon juice in a bowl and whisk to a smooth consistency.

Slowly mix in grated cucumber to blend well, and season with salt. Serve chilled.

Serves 4

hot & sour tomato soup

see variations page 57

Try this classic favourite with a twist for some added kick and tang.

1 tbsp light cooking oil
1 medium-sized onion, thinly sliced
2.5-cm (1-in) chunk of ginger
2–3 large cloves of garlic
$^1/_4$ tsp red chilli powder
$^1/_4$ tsp turmeric powder
$^1/_4$ tsp coriander powder
2 medium-sized tomatoes, chopped

about 1 l (34 fl oz) chicken or vegetable stock
2 stalks lemongrass, lightly bruised
    and roughly broken into pieces
1–2 large red chillies, seeds included,
    sliced in 2.5-cm (1-in) pieces
salt and pepper, to taste
1 tbsp fresh lemon juice

Heat oil in a deep pan and sauté onions, ginger and garlic until tender. Add in chilli, turmeric and coriander powders, and fry for a few seconds before adding in the tomatoes. Fry, stirring occasionally, until the tomatoes start to pulp.

Add in chicken or vegetable broth, lemongrass and sliced chillies. Let the soup come to the boil, then allow it to simmer for 15 minutes. Season with salt and pepper.

Serves 4

coconut & sweetcorn soup

see variations page 58

This light, creamy soup gives a wonderful taste of south India and is perfect for when you're craving something comforting.

1 tbsp light cooking oil
1 tbsp crushed garlic
1 tbsp ready-made curry paste
1 small onion, thinly sliced
240 ml (8 fl oz) coconut milk
750 ml (25 fl oz) chicken or vegetable stock

1 stalk lemongrass, bruised and cut
   into 5-cm (2-in) pieces
140 g (5 oz) frozen sweetcorn, thawed
salt and pepper, to taste
fresh coriander leaves and green chillies,
   chopped, for garnish
lemon wedges

Heat oil in a deep pan and sauté garlic and curry paste for a few seconds until fragrant. Add in onions and sauté until lightly browned.

Add coconut milk, broth and lemongrass, and let soup come to the boil on a low heat. Add in sweetcorn and leave to simmer for 5–10 minutes.

Season with salt and pepper, and garnish with coriander leaves and green chillies. Serve with lemon wedges.

Serves 4

lentil soup

see variations page 59

Flavoured with aromatic cumin and fennel seeds, this is a delicious and healthy soup to warm up a chilly evening.

200 g (7 oz) dried red lentils, washed
    and drained
500 ml (17 fl oz) water
1 small onion, chopped
1 small tomato, chopped
2 large garlic cloves

2.5-cm (1-in) piece of ginger, chopped
$^1/_4$ tsp turmeric powder
$^1/_4$ tsp red chilli powder
1 tbsp oil
$^1/_2$ tsp cumin seeds
$^1/_2$ tsp fennel seeds

In a large pan, boil lentils in water along with onions, tomatoes, garlic and ginger, turmeric and chilli powders, until lentils start to soften and become mushy. Allow to cool to room temperature before blending mixture to a smooth consistency in a blender. Return soup to the pan.

In a small pan, heat oil and sauté cumin and fennel seeds until they start to sizzle. Add the toasted cumin and fennel seeds, along with the oil, to the soup and let it come to the boil. Season with salt.

Serves 4

variations

fish cutlets

see base recipe page 17

tuna cutlets
Prepare the basic recipe, substituting 225 g (8 oz) tinned flaked tuna in water for the fish. Rinse and drain before using.

prawn cutlets
Prepare the basic recipe, substituting 340 g (12 oz) shelled and deveined prawns for the fish.

chicken cutlets
Prepare the basic recipe, substituting 140 g (5 oz) ground chicken for the fish. Cook for 10 minutes more or until chicken is completely cooked through.

lamb cutlets
Prepare the basic recipe, substituting 225 g (8 oz) ground lamb for the fish. Cook for 10 minutes more or until lamb is cooked through.

variations

masala meatballs

see base recipe page 18

minty meatballs
Prepare the basic recipe, adding in 1 tablespoon dried mint along with the rest of the spices.

sesame meatballs
Prepare the basic recipe, dipping the meatballs in a bowl of sesame seeds to coat all over before frying.

fennel meatballs
Prepare the basic recipe, adding in 1 tablespoon crushed fennel seeds along with the rest of the spices.

cardamom meatballs
Prepare the basic recipe, adding in $\frac{1}{2}$ teaspoon crushed cardamom seeds along with the rest of the spices.

pepper meatballs
Prepare the basic recipe, adding in 1 teaspoon crushed black peppercorns along with the rest of the spices.

gobi manchurian

see base recipe page 20

paneer manchurian

Prepare the basic recipe, substituting 375 g (13 oz) paneer, cubed, for the cauliflower florets.

mushroom manchurian

Prepare the basic recipe, substituting 340 g (12 oz) baby button mushrooms for the cauliflower florets.

potato manchurian

Prepare the basic recipe, substituting 675 g (24 oz) cubed potatoes for the cauliflower florets.

baby sweetcorn manchurian

Prepare the basic recipe, substituting 400g (14 oz) tinned baby sweetcorn for the cauliflower florets. Rinse and drain sweetcorn. Reduce salt in recipe.

broccoli manchurian

Prepare the basic recipe, substituting 400 g (14 oz) uncooked broccoli for the cauliflower florets.

variations

spicy potato wedges

see base recipe page 23

fennel potato wedges
Prepare the basic recipe, adding in 1 tablespoon crushed fennel seeds along with the rest of the spices.

sesame potato wedges
Prepare the basic recipe, adding in 1 tablespoon sesame seeds along with the rest of the spices.

lemony potato wedges
Prepare the basic recipe, adding in 1 tablespoon lemon zest along with the rest of the spices.

peppery potato wedges
Prepare the basic recipe, adding in 1 teaspoon crushed black peppercorns along with the rest of the spices.

garlic potato wedges
Instead of the spices used in the base recipe, use 1 tablespoon minced garlic along with oil and a pinch of salt. Follow the recipe as directed.

coriander paneer pakodas

see base recipe page 25

mint paneer pakodas

Prepare the basic recipe, substituting 140 g (5 oz) mint for the coriander.

dill paneer pakodas

Prepare the basic recipe, substituting 140 g (5 oz) dill for the coriander.

spinach paneer pakodas

Prepare the basic recipe, substituting 140 g (5 oz) fresh spinach for the coriander.

tomato paneer pakodas

Prepare the basic recipe, substituting 140 g (5 oz) de-seeded tomatoes for the coriander. Don't add water in the blender.

coriander potato pakodas

Prepare the basic recipe, substituting 400 g (14 oz) thin slices of potato for the paneer.

coriander aubergine pakodas

Prepare the basic recipe, substituting 400 g (14 oz) thin slices of aubergine for the paneer.

coriander courgette pakodas

Prepare the basic recipe, substituting 400 g (14 oz) thin slices of courgette for the paneer.

variations

samosas

see base recipe page 26

sweet potato samosas
Prepare the basic recipe, substituting 260 g (9 oz) sweet potatoes for the potatoes. Omit the peas.

carrot & pea samosas
Prepare the basic recipe, substituting 260 g (9 oz) carrots for the potatoes.

cauliflower samosas
Prepare basic recipe, substituting 260 g (9 oz) cauliflower florets for potatoes.

minty potato samosas
Prepare the basic recipe, substituting 2 tablespoons fresh mint for the coriander seeds and powder. Omit the peas.

lemony potato samosas
Prepare the basic recipe, substituting 1 tablespoon lemon zest for the coriander seeds and powder. Omit the peas.

dill potato samosas
Prepare the basic recipe, substituting 2 tablespoons fresh dill for the coriander seeds and powder. Omit the peas.

variations

fish pakodas

see base recipe page 28

sesame fish pakodas

Prepare the basic recipe, adding 1 tablespoon sesame seeds to the batter.

minty fish pakodas

Prepare the basic recipe, adding 1 tablespoon dried mint to the batter.

chicken pakodas

Prepare the basic recipe, substituting 450 g (1 lb) chicken breast for the fish.

prawns pakodas

Prepare the basic recipe, substituting 450 g (1 lb) peeled and deveined prawns for the fish.

potato pakodas

Prepare the basic recipe, substituting 400 g (14 oz) thin slices of peeled potatoes for the fish.

aubergine pakodas

Prepare the basic recipe, substituting 400 g (14 oz) thin slices of aubergine for the fish.

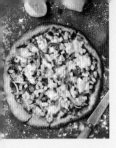

variations

paneer tikka pizza

see base recipe page 31

chicken tikka pizza

Substitute 1 medium-sized chicken breast, chopped into bite-sized pieces, for the paneer. Follow the recipe as directed, but sauté the marinated chicken in 1 tablespoon cooking oil until it starts to brown along the edges, before adding it onto the pizza.

mushroom tikka pizza

Prepare the basic recipe, substituting 140 g (5 oz) sliced mushrooms for the paneer.

cauliflower tikka pizza

Prepare the basic recipe, substituting 140 g (5 oz) bite-sized cauliflower florets for the paneer.

variations

masala chicken wings

see base recipe page 32

lemony chicken wings
Prepare the basic recipe, adding in 1 tablespoon lemon zest along with the rest of the spices.

minty chicken wings
Prepare the basic recipe, adding in 1 tablespoon dried mint along with the rest of the spices.

fennel chicken wings
Prepare the basic recipe, adding in 1 tablespoon crushed fennel seeds along with the rest of the spices.

curry leaf chicken wings
Prepare the basic recipe, adding in 1 tablespoon crushed dried curry leaves along with the rest of the spices.

peppery chicken wings
Prepare the basic recipe, adding in 1 tablespoon crushed black peppercorns along with the rest of the spices.

variations

paneer croquettes

see base recipe page 35

minty croquettes
Prepare the basic recipe, adding in 1 tablespoon dried mint along with the rest of the spices.

fennel croquettes
Prepare the basic recipe, adding in 1 tablespoon fennel seeds along with the rest of the spices.

sesame croquettes
Prepare the basic recipe, adding in 1 tablespoon sesame seeds along with the rest of the spices.

peppery croquettes
Prepare the basic recipe, adding in 1 tablespoon crushed black peppercorns along with the rest of the spices.

cumin croquettes
Prepare the basic recipe, adding in 1 tablespoon crushed roasted cumin seeds along with the rest of the spices. Omit cumin powder.

curried carrot soup

see base recipe page 36

minty carrot soup
Prepare the basic recipe, substituting 1 teaspoon dried mint for parsley.

fennel carrot soup
Prepare basic recipe, substituting 1 teaspoon crushed fennel seeds for parsley.

peppery carrot soup
Prepare the basic recipe, substituting 1 teaspoon crushed black peppercorns for parsley.

curried sweet potato soup
Prepare the basic recipe, substituting 260 g (9 oz) sweet potatoes for the carrots.

curried pea soup
Prepare the basic recipe, substituting 300 g (11 oz) thawed frozen peas for the carrots.

minty pea soup
Prepare the basic recipe, substituting 1 teaspoon dried mint for the parsley and 260 g (9 oz) thawed frozen peas for the carrots.

variations

cucumber & yoghurt soup

see base recipe page 39

carrot & yoghurt soup
Prepare basic recipe, substituting 140 g (5 oz) grated carrots for cucumber.

beetroot & yoghurt soup
Prepare basic recipe, substituting 140 g (5 oz) grated beetroot for cucumber.

veggie yoghurt soup
Prepare the basic recipe, adding in 140 g (5 oz) chopped tomatoes, onions and shredded carrots with the cucumber.

potato & yoghurt soup
Prepare the basic recipe, substituting 140 g (5 oz) grated boiled potatoes for the cucumber.

minty cucumber soup
Prepare the basic recipe, substituting 2 tablespoons fresh mint for the coriander leaves.

dill & cucumber soup
Prepare basic recipe, substituting 2 tablespoons fresh dill for coriander leaves.

variations

hot & sour tomato soup

see base recipe page 40

tomato rice soup

Prepare the basic recipe, adding in 140 g (5 oz) rice along with the stock.
Increase simmering time by 10 minutes or until the rice is cooked.

hot & sour mushroom soup

Prepare the basic recipe, adding in 140 g (5 oz) sliced mushrooms along with
the chopped tomatoes.

hot & sour tofu soup

Prepare the basic recipe, adding in 140 g (5 oz) chopped firm tofu along with
the chopped tomatoes.

hot & sour chicken soup

Prepare the basic recipe, adding in 140 g (5 oz) chopped boneless chicken along
with the chopped tomatoes. Increase simmering time by 10 minutes or until the
chicken is cooked through.

hot & sour veggie soup

Prepare the basic recipe, adding in 140 g (5 oz) chopped mixed vegetables, like
carrots, peas and sweetcorn, along with the chopped tomatoes.

variations

coconut & sweetcorn soup

see base recipe page 43

coconut & prawn soup
Prepare the basic recipe, adding 140 g (5 oz) shelled and deveined prawns
along with the onions. Increase simmering time by 10 minutes or until the
prawns are completely cooked through.

coconut & tofu soup
Prepare the basic recipe, adding 140 g (5 oz) chopped firm tofu along with the
onions. Increase simmering time by 10 minutes.

coconut & chicken soup
Prepare the basic recipe, adding 140 g (5 oz) chopped boneless chicken along
with the onions. Increase simmering time by 10 minutes or until the chicken is
completely cooked through.

coconut & fish soup
Prepare the basic recipe, adding 140 g (5 oz) chopped firm fish along with the
onions. Increase simmering time by 10 minutes or until the fish is completely
cooked through.

coconut & tomato soup
Prepare basic recipe, adding 140 g (5 oz) chopped tomatoes with the onions.

variations

lentil soup

see base recipe page 44

chickpea soup

Prepare the basic recipe, substituting 260 g (9 oz) cooked chickpeas for the lentils.

kidney bean soup

Prepare the basic recipe, substituting 260 g (9 oz) cooked red kidney beans for the lentils. If red kidney beans are tinned, rinse and drain, and omit salt from recipe.

black bean soup

Prepare the basic recipe, substituting 260 g (9 oz) cooked black beans for the lentils. If black beans are tinned, rinse and drain, and omit salt from recipe.

pea soup

Prepare the basic recipe, substituting 140 g (5 oz) peas for the lentils.

sweetcorn soup

Prepare basic recipe, substituting 140 g (5 oz) sweetcorn for the lentils.

cauliflower soup

Prepare basic recipe, substituting 140 g (5 oz) chopped cauliflower for lentils.

kebabs

There's no better way to entertain than to fire up the grill and lay out a delicious spread. Traditional Indian cooking often uses a *tandoor* – a clay oven fuelled by wood or charcoal, but these scrumptious treats will work just as well on a home barbecue.

chicken kebabs

see variations page 77

These kebabs can be enjoyed on their own with a yoghurt dip. However, I often like to chop them into tiny pieces and wrap them into a warm tortilla with lettuce and tomatoes for a quick, filling lunch.

2 chicken breasts (about 450 g/1 lb total),
    cut into 2.5-cm (1-in) cubes
140g (5 oz) natural yoghurt, full fat or low fat,
    beaten until smooth
1 tbsp light cooking oil
2 tbsp fresh lemon juice
1 tsp minced garlic
1 tsp minced ginger

$\frac{1}{2}$ tsp red chilli powder
$\frac{1}{2}$ tsp coriander powder
$\frac{1}{2}$ tsp cumin powder
$\frac{1}{4}$ tsp garam masala
$\frac{1}{4}$ tsp amchur powder
salt, to taste
light cooking oil for pan

Mix chicken pieces with the rest of the ingredients in a bowl to coat well, and marinate for at least 4 hours in a fridge.

Line up chicken cubes on an oiled, heated griddle and cook on the hob for 3–5 minutes; then turn so they cook on all sides, and cook for another 5 minutes, until chicken is cooked through and shows griddle marks. Alternatively, you can bake the chicken in an oven preheated to 200°C/Gas Mark 6 (400°F) for 15–20 minutes, turning once.

Serves 4

stuffed tandoori mushrooms

see variations page 78

These are perfect finger food to pass around a party; they are amazing served either warm or at room temperature.

1 tbsp light cooking oil
1 tsp cumin seeds
1 tbsp minced garlic
1 medium-sized onion, finely chopped
$1/4$ tsp red chilli powder
$1/2$ tsp coriander powder
$1/4$ tsp cumin powder
salt, to taste
2 tbsp fresh coriander leaves, finely chopped

12–15 baby portobello or white button
    mushrooms (about 450 g/1 lb),
    stems removed
260 g (9 oz) natural yoghurt, full fat or low fat,
    beaten until smooth
1 tsp garam masala
1 tsp amchur powder
2 tbsp fresh lemon juice
salt, to taste
light cooking oil for pan

Sauté the cumin and garlic in hot oil until they start to sizzle. Add in onions, chilli, coriander and cumin powders and salt, and fry for a few minutes, until onions soften and are lightly browned. Mix in coriander leaves and set aside to cool.

In the meantime, marinate mushrooms in yoghurt, garam masala, amchur powder, lemon juice and salt for about half an hour. Preheat oven to 200°C/Gas Mark 6 (400°F). Take mushrooms out of the marinade, discarding any excess, and stuff each with about 1 tablespoon of onion mix. Bake on an oiled baking tray for 15–20 minutes, until the filling of the mushrooms starts to brown and the mushrooms are cooked through.

Serves 4

tandoori prawns

see variations page 79

For best results, make sure to use fresh prawns, as they are packed with flavour. If you are in a hurry, you can also pan fry the prawns on a high heat until they turn opaque and are cooked through.

15–20 large prawns (about 900 g/2 lbs),
    peeled and deveined
2 tbsp tomato paste
1 tbsp fresh lemon juice
1 tbsp light cooking oil
1 tsp garlic powder
$\frac{1}{2}$ tsp red chilli powder

$\frac{1}{2}$ tsp amchur powder
$\frac{1}{4}$ tsp turmeric powder
salt and pepper, to taste
light cooking oil for pan
fresh lemon slice for garnish

Mix together all the ingredients except the lemon juice and oil for the pan, and then mix in the prawns to coat well. Leave the prawns to sit and marinate for 15–20 minutes.

Place marinated prawns on a heated, lightly oiled griddle and cook on the hob for 2–3 minutes on each side, until they turn crisp and are cooked through.

Drizzle with fresh lemon juice and serve.

Serves 4

minty fish tikka

see variations page 80

This recipe is wonderful served as an appetiser or as part of a tapas menu. It is a breeze to prepare and takes absolutely no time to cook.

2 large boneless fillets (about 450 g/1 lb total)
  of any firm white fish, cut into 2.5-cm
  (1-in) square pieces
1 tbsp fresh coriander leaves, finely chopped
2 tbsp fresh mint leaves, finely chopped
1 tbsp fresh lemon juice
2 tbsp light cooking oil

1 tsp garlic powder
$^{1}/_{2}$ tsp red chilli powder
$^{1}/_{4}$ tsp cumin powder
$^{1}/_{4}$ tsp amchur powder
salt, to taste
light cooking oil for pan

In a bowl, mix together everything except the fish and oil for the pan, and then mix in the fish pieces and marinate for 15–20 minutes in the fridge.

Place marinated fish on an oiled, heated griddle and cook on the hob for 2–3 minutes on each side, until the fish turns crisp and is cooked through.

Serves 4

green cutlets

see variations page 81

You can serve these on their own with a dip on the side, or make a complete meal of them with the addition of some naans and a light salad.

2 large potatoes, peeled, boiled and mashed
140 g (5 oz) frozen peas, thawed and mashed
1 small onion, finely chopped
1 tsp garlic powder
$\frac{1}{2}$ tsp red chilli powder
$\frac{1}{2}$ tsp coriander powder

$\frac{1}{2}$ tsp chaat masala
$\frac{1}{4}$ tsp garam masala
2 tbsp fresh lemon juice
salt, to taste
light cooking oil for frying

Mix potatoes, peas, onion, spices, lemon juice and salt, and form into golf-ball-sized balls. Gently flatten out each ball to form patties, and smooth out edges.

Heat oil in a frying pan, and shallow-fry the patties until golden and crisp on each side.

Serves 4

lamb chops

see variations page 82

For this recipe, it is important to marinate the lamb for as long as possible to infuse maximum flavour. The marinated meat can easily be frozen for later use, and an extra batch can be saved for a busy day.

6–8 lamb chops (about 900 g/2 lbs),
   French-boned
260 g (9 oz) natural yoghurt, full fat or low fat,
   beaten until smooth
1 tbsp minced garlic
1 tbsp minced ginger
2 tbsp fresh coriander leaves,
   finely chopped
2 tbsp fresh lemon juice

2 tbsp light cooking oil
$\frac{1}{2}$ tsp red chilli powder
$\frac{1}{2}$ tsp chaat masala
$\frac{1}{2}$ tsp garam masala
1 tsp coriander powder
1 tsp cumin powder
salt, to taste
light cooking oil for baking tray

Mix all ingredients, except salt and oil for the baking tray, together and marinate lamb chops in the mixture for at least 2 hours. Towards the end, preheat oven to 200°C/Gas Mark 6 (400°F).

Place lamb chops on an oiled baking tray and bake in the oven for 20–30 minutes, turning them once, until the meat is tender and cooked through.

Serves 4

lamb tikkas

see variations page 83

Serve these tikkas with sides of naans and raita for a simple dinner, or pair them with a choice of curries, salad and pulao for a more exotic meal.

900 g (2 lbs) boneless leg of lamb,
    cut into 2.5-cm (1-in) cubes
260 g (9 oz) natural yoghurt, full fat or
    low fat, beaten until smooth
2 tbsp fresh coriander leaves,
    finely chopped
2 tbsp fresh mint leaves,
    finely chopped
1 tsp minced garlic

1 tsp minced ginger
$^1/_2$ tsp red chilli powder
$^1/_2$ tsp amchur powder
1 tsp garam masala
2 tbsp fresh lemon juice
2 tbsp light cooking oil
salt, to taste
light cooking oil for
    baking tray

Mix all ingredients, except lamb and oil for the baking tray, together and marinate the meat in them, in the fridge, for at least 2 hours. Towards the end, preheat oven to 200°C/Gas Mark 6 (400°F).

Place lamb pieces on an oiled baking tray in the oven and bake for 20–30 minutes, turning once, until the meat is tender and cooked through.

Serves 4

tandoori chicken legs

see variations page 84

Tandoori chicken is one of the most popular dishes in Indian cuisine. The flavours of the traditional dish are fairly easy to recreate and the chicken legs cook extremely well in a regular convection oven or over a barbecue.

8–10 skinless chicken drumsticks,
   slit on the sides
1 tbsp minced garlic
1 tbsp minced ginger
1 tbsp light cooking oil
1 tbsp yoghurt, full fat or low fat,
   beaten until smooth
2 tbsp lemon juice

$\frac{1}{4}$ tsp turmeric powder
$\frac{1}{2}$ tsp red chilli powder
1 tsp coriander powder
1 tsp cumin powder
1 tsp garam masala
salt, to taste
light cooking oil for pan

Mix together all the ingredients except the chicken and oil for the pan, and then mix in the chicken, coating it thoroughly. Leave the drumsticks to marinate for at least an hour in the fridge. Towards the end, preheat the oven to 190°C/Gas Mark 5 (375°F).

Place chicken on an oiled grill pan and cook in the oven for 20–25 minutes, turning once, until chicken is tender and cooked through.

Serves 4

paneer shashlik

see variations page 85

Paneer is a soft cheese that maintains its shape and doesn't melt at a high heat. Hence it is often used as a perfect alternative to chicken or meat for vegetarians in Indian cuisine.

450 g (1 lb) paneer, cut into 2.5-cm
  (1-in) cubes
140g (5 oz) natural yoghurt, full fat or low fat,
  beaten until smooth
$\frac{1}{4}$ tsp red chilli powder
$\frac{1}{2}$ tsp amchur powder
$\frac{1}{2}$ tsp garlic powder
$\frac{1}{2}$ tsp coriander powder
$\frac{1}{2}$ tsp cumin powder
1 tbsp fresh lemon juice

1 tbsp light cooking oil
salt, to taste
bamboo skewers, soaked in water
  for at least 20 minutes
1 medium-sized green pepper,
  cut into 2.5-cm (1-in) pieces
1 medium-sized onion, cut into
  2.5-cm (1-in) pieces
light cooking oil for pan

Marinate paneer in a mixture of the yoghurt, spices, lemon juice, oil and salt, and place in fridge to marinate for 30 minutes.

Skewer marinated paneer pieces, alternating with green pepper and onion pieces, and place on a hot grill pan; fry for 2–3 minutes on each side until paneer crisps up and is cooked through.

Serves 4

variations

chicken kebabs

see base recipe page 61

minty chicken kebabs
Prepare the basic recipe, adding in 1 tablespoon dried mint leaves along with
the spices.

lemon chicken kebabs
Prepare the basic recipe, adding in 1 tablespoon lemon zest along with
the spices.

fennel chicken kebabs
Prepare the basic recipe, adding in 1 tablespoon crushed fennel seeds along
with the spices.

sesame chicken kebabs
Prepare the basic recipe, adding in 1 tablespoon sesame seeds along with
the spices.

potato kebabs
Prepare the basic recipe, substituting 340 g (12 oz) peeled baby potatoes for the
chicken. Increase cooking time by 5 minutes.

variations

stuffed tandoori mushrooms

see base recipe page 62

minty stuffed mushrooms
Prepare the basic recipe, substituting 2 tablespoons fresh mint leaves for the coriander leaves.

dill-stuffed mushrooms
Prepare the basic recipe, substituting 2 tablespoons fresh dill for the coriander leaves.

fennel-stuffed mushrooms
Prepare the basic recipe, adding in 1 tablespoon fennel seeds along with the rest of the spices.

sesame-stuffed mushrooms
Prepare the basic recipe, adding in 1 tablespoon sesame seeds along with the rest of the spices.

variations

tandoori prawns

see base recipe page 64

tandoori chicken
Prepare the basic recipe, substituting 450 g (1 lb) cubed boneless chicken breast for prawns. Increase cooking time by 10 minutes or until the chicken is completely cooked through.

tandoori fish
Prepare the basic recipe, substituting 450 g (1 lb) cubed firm white fish for the prawns. Increase cooking time by 10 minutes or until the fish is completely cooked through.

tandoori paneer
Prepare the basic recipe, substituting 280 g (10 oz) cubed paneer for the prawns. Decrease cooking time by 5 minutes.

tandoori potatoes
Prepare the basic recipe, substituting 340 g (12 oz) peeled baby potatoes for the prawns. Increase cooking time by 10 minutes.

tandoori mushrooms
Prepare the basic recipe, substituting 280 g (10 oz) button mushrooms for the prawns. Decrease cooking time by 5 minutes.

variations

minty fish tikka

see base recipe page 67

dill fish tikka
Prepare the basic recipe, substituting 2 tablespoons chopped fresh dill for the mint.

fennel fish tikka
Prepare the basic recipe, substituting 1 tablespoon crushed fennel seeds for the mint.

sesame fish tikka
Prepare the basic recipe, substituting 1 tablespoon sesame seeds for the mint.

minty chicken tikka
Prepare the basic recipe, substituting 450 g (1 lb) cubed boneless chicken breast for the fish. Increase cooking time by 10 minutes, or until chicken is completely cooked through.

minty paneer tikka
Prepare the basic recipe, substituting 280 g (10 oz) cubed paneer for the fish. Decrease cooking time by 5 minutes.

variations

green cutlets

see base recipe page 68

green paneer cutlets

Prepare the basic recipe, substituting 60 g (2 oz) crumbled paneer for one of the potatoes.

green chicken cutlets

Prepare the basic recipe, substituting 140 g (5 oz) minced chicken for one of the potatoes. Fry for 10 minutes more, or until chicken is completely cooked through.

green lamb cutlets

Prepare the basic recipe, substituting 140 g (5 oz) minced lamb for one of the potatoes. Fry for 10 minutes more, or until lamb is completely cooked through.

green tuna cutlets

Prepare the basic recipe, substituting 200 g (7 oz) of tinned tuna in water, rinsed, drained and crumbled, for one of the potatoes. Fry for 5 minutes more.

green veggie cutlets

Prepare the basic recipe, substituting 170 g (6 oz) grated steamed cauliflower for one of the potatoes.

variations

lamb chops

see base recipe page 70

minty lamb chops
Prepare the basic recipe, substituting 2 tablespoons fresh mint leaves for the coriander.

dill lamb chops
Prepare the basic recipe, substituting 2 tablespoons fresh dill for the coriander.

fennel lamb chops
Prepare the basic recipe, adding in 1 tablespoon fennel seeds along with the rest of the spices.

sesame lamb chops
Prepare the basic recipe, adding in 1 tablespoon sesame seeds along with the rest of the spices.

peppery lamb chops
Prepare the basic recipe, adding in 1 tablespoon crushed black peppercorns along with the rest of the spices.

variations

lamb tikkas

see base recipe page 73

dill lamb tikkas
Prepare the basic recipe, substituting 2 tablespoons fresh dill for the coriander and mint.

fennel lamb tikkas
Prepare the basic recipe, adding in 1 tablespoon fennel seeds along with the rest of the spices.

sesame lamb tikkas
Prepare the basic recipe, adding in 1 tablespoon sesame seeds along with the rest of the spices.

peppery lamb tikkas
Prepare the basic recipe, adding in 1 tablespoon crushed peppercorns along with the rest of the spices.

lemony lamb tikkas
Prepare the basic recipe, adding in 1 tablespoon lemon zest along with the rest of the spices.

variations

tandoori chicken legs

see base recipe page 74

lemony chicken legs
Prepare the basic recipe, adding in 1 tablespoon lemon zest along with the rest of the spices.

minty chicken legs
Prepare the basic recipe, adding in 1 tablespoon dried mint along with the rest of the spices.

fennel chicken legs
Prepare the basic recipe, adding in 1 tablespoon crushed fennel seeds along with the rest of the spices.

curry leaf chicken legs
Prepare the basic recipe, adding in 1 tablespoon dried crushed curry leaves along with the rest of the spices.

tandoori chicken breasts
Prepare the basic recipe, substituting 4 butterflied chicken breasts for the chicken legs. Check the chicken breasts after 15–20 minutes.

variations

paneer shashlik

see base recipe page 76

chicken shashlik
Prepare the basic recipe, substituting 450 g (1 lb) cubed boneless chicken breast for the paneer. Adjust cooking time accordingly.

mushroom shashlik
Prepare the basic recipe, substituting 280 g (10 oz) button mushrooms for the paneer. Adjust cooking time accordingly.

potato shashlik
Prepare the basic recipe, substituting 340 g (12 oz) boiled baby potatoes for the paneer. Adjust cooking time accordingly.

cauliflower shashlik
Prepare the basic recipe, substituting 340 g (12 oz) cauliflower florets for the paneer. Adjust cooking time accordingly.

chicken

Chicken is great when you don't want to slave over the stove for too long. Indian spices can quickly transform it into a taste sensation – try these mouth-watering recipes for a new twist to your dinners.

chicken tikka masala

see variations page 102

Try this quick, modern twist on a classic restaurant favourite.

2 large boneless chicken breasts (about 450 g/
    1lb) cut into 2.5-cm (1-in) cubes
260 g (9 oz) natural yoghurt, full fat or low fat,
    beaten until smooth
1 tsp minced garlic
1 tsp minced ginger
$\frac{1}{2}$ tsp red chilli powder
$\frac{1}{2}$ tsp amchur powder

1 tsp garam masala
2 tbsp light cooking oil
225 g (8 oz) pureed fresh tomatoes (from about
    3 medium-sized tomatoes)
2 tbsp tomato paste
1 tsp ground cashews
1 tsp kasoori methi (dried fenugreek leaves)
salt, to taste

Marinate chicken in a mixture of the yoghurt, garlic, ginger, chilli powder, amchur powder, garam masala and salt, and let it sit for at least an hour.

Heat oil in heavy-bottomed pan, and add in the meat with all the marinade. Cook chicken, stirring occasionally, for 5–8 minutes, until it starts to firm up and the yoghurt marinade begins to dry. Add in pureed tomatoes, tomato paste, ground cashews and kasoori methi, and cook, covered, for 10–15 minutes. Season with salt.

Serves 4

home-style chicken curry

see variations page 103

Curries can be a quick go-to solution when you don't have too much time to
fuss over dinner. They are best enjoyed with a side of plain white rice or the
Indian bread called roti, served warm.

2 tbsp light cooking oil
1 cinnamon stick, 5-cm (2-in) long
1–2 dried bay leaves
5–6 whole cloves
3–4 green cardamom pods, lightly bruised
5–6 black peppercorns
1 tsp cumin seeds
1 large onion, finely chopped
1 tbsp minced garlic
1 tbsp minced ginger
$\frac{1}{4}$ tsp turmeric powder
$\frac{1}{2}$ tsp red chilli powder
1 tsp cumin powder

1 tsp coriander powder
$\frac{1}{2}$ tsp garam masala
2 medium-sized tomatoes, finely chopped
140 g (5 oz) natural yoghurt, full fat or low fat,
    beaten until smooth
2 large chicken breasts (about 450 g/1 lb),
    cubed
water, as needed
salt, to taste
fresh coriander leaves, finely chopped,
    for garnish

Heat oil in a heavy-bottomed pan and sauté cinnamon stick, bay leaves, cloves, cardamom
and peppercorns, until they begin to sizzle. Add cumin seeds and onions, and fry for
3–5 minutes, until onions turn pink and tender. Add garlic and ginger, and sauté for
another minute or two, until fragrant.

Add in the rest of the spices, and fry for a minute. Mix in chopped tomatoes and cook for
a few minutes, until tomatoes pulp and the mixture releases oil around the sides of the pan.

With the heat on low, slowly stir in beaten yoghurt, forming a smooth gravy base.

Add in chicken cubes; add water if necessary to get desired consistency and salt, and allow to cook, covered, for 10–15 minutes on a medium-low heat until chicken is cooked through.

Garnish with chopped coriander leaves and serve piping hot.
Serves 4

green chicken curry

see variations page 104

Coriander leaves are regularly used as a garnish on Indian curries, but using them as a base for the curry itself brings out a whole new side of this popular herb.

30 g (1 oz) fresh coriander leaves,
    roughly chopped
2 tbsp light cooking oil
1 tsp cumin seeds
1 small onion, thinly sliced
1 tsp minced ginger
1 tsp minced garlic
$\frac{1}{2}$ tsp red chilli powder
$\frac{1}{2}$ tsp coriander powder

$\frac{1}{2}$ tsp garam masala
1 tsp cumin powder
140 g (5 oz) natural yoghurt, beaten
    until smooth
2 large chicken breasts (about 450 g/1 lb),
    sliced into 0.5-cm ($\frac{1}{8}$-in) strips
water as needed
salt, to taste

In a blender, blend the coriander leaves into a smooth paste. Set aside. Heat oil in a heavy saucepan and sauté cumin seeds, onions, ginger and garlic for a few minutes until onions start to soften.

Add in chilli and coriander powders, garam masala and cumin powder, and fry for a few seconds before adding in the coriander paste. Once the spices have mixed well with the paste, add in yoghurt and cook for a minute or two.

Add the chicken, plus a little water, if necessary, depending on the consistency of curry you like, and let it come to a boil. Season with salt and let the curry simmer, uncovered, for another 6–8 minutes, until chicken is completely cooked through.

Serves 4

kadhai chicken

see variations page 105

A *kadhai* is a deep, circular cooking pan, similar to a wok, with circular handles on either side. It is a basic tool of Indian cooking. Kadhai chicken is a drier version of regular curry; it is best enjoyed with warm roti, the traditional Indian bread.

2 tbsp light cooking oil
1 tsp cumin seeds
1 tsp coriander seeds
1 medium-sized onion, chopped
1 tbsp minced ginger
1/2 tsp red chilli powder
1/4 tsp turmeric powder
1 tsp coriander powder

1/4 tsp garam masala
2 large boneless chicken breasts (about 450 g/
    1lb), sliced into 0.5-cm (1/8-in) thick strips
1 large tomato, chopped
salt, to taste
2 tbsp fresh coriander leaves, finely chopped,
    for garnish

Heat oil in a large deep wok, and sauté cumin and coriander seeds until they start to sizzle. Add in onions and ginger and fry for a few minutes until tender.

Add in chilli, turmeric and coriander powders and garam masala, and fry for a few seconds before adding in the chicken. Stir fry the meat to coat well with the spices. Add in tomatoes and salt, and leave the chicken to cook, covered, for 5–6 minutes, until completely done.

Garnish with coriander leaves.

Serves 4

chicken & chickpea curry

see variations page 106

Make this dish on cold winter nights when you're yearning for something hearty and comforting.

2 tbsp light cooking oil
1 large onion, thinly sliced
1 tbsp ginger, finely chopped
1 tbsp garlic, finely chopped
1 tbsp green chillies, finely chopped
$1/4$ tsp red chilli powder
$1/4$ tsp turmeric powder
$1/4$ tsp cumin powder
1 tsp coriander powder
$1/2$ tsp garam masala

140 g (5 oz) natural yoghurt, full fat or low fat
2 boneless chicken breasts (about 450 g/1 lb), cut into 2.5-cm (1-in) cubes
170 g (6 oz) cooked chickpeas, fresh or tinned, rinsed thoroughly and drained
water, as needed
1 tbsp kasoori methi (dried fenugreek leaves)
salt, to taste

Heat oil and fry onions, along with ginger, garlic and green chillies, until they begin to brown. Add in chilli, turmeric, cumin and coriander powders and garam masala, and fry for a few seconds.

Slowly mix in yoghurt and cook for a few minutes until it is well blended with the spices. Add in chicken cubes and chickpeas, and mix well. Add water if needed to get the curry consistency you like, and cook, covered, for 10–12 minutes.

Add kasoori methi and salt, and cook, covered, for another 5–7 minutes.

Serves 4

chicken masala

see variations page 107

A *masala* is a mixture of spices. Although the spice level is not too high in this dish, the undertones of the spices provide that much-needed depth in a curry. Serve it with an aromatic pulao and some cool raita on the side.

2 tbsp light cooking oil
1 tsp cumin seeds
120 g (4 oz) onions, thinly sliced
1–2 green chillies, including seeds,
    finely chopped
$\frac{1}{2}$ tsp red chilli powder
$\frac{1}{2}$ tsp cumin powder
$\frac{1}{4}$ tsp turmeric powder
1 tbsp coriander powder

200g (7 oz) chopped tomatoes (from about
    2 medium-sized tomatoes)
2 boneless chicken breasts (about 450 g/1 lb),
    cut into 2.5-cm (1-in) cubes
$\frac{1}{2}$ tsp garam masala
salt, to taste
fresh coriander leaves, chopped,
    for garnish

Heat oil in a deep pan and add cumin seeds. Wait until they start to sizzle; then add sliced onions and green chillies. Fry until onions are lightly browned.

Add in chilli, cumin, turmeric and coriander powders and tomatoes, and cook for a few minutes, until tomatoes begin to pulp. Add in chicken cubes and cook, covered, for 8–10 minutes.

Sprinkle with garam masala and salt, and cook for another 5–6 minutes, covered, until chicken is done. Garnish with chopped coriander leaves.

Serves 4

mango chicken curry

see variations page 108

India is well known throughout the world for its abundance of delicious, juicy mangoes. The mango in this curry adds a delightful freshness to a simple everyday meal.

2 tbsp light cooking oil
1 medium-sized onion, sliced
1–2 red chillies, including seeds, finely chopped
1 tsp minced ginger
$\frac{1}{4}$ tsp turmeric powder
$\frac{1}{2}$ tsp red chilli powder
$\frac{1}{2}$ tsp cumin powder

$\frac{1}{2}$ tsp coriander powder
2 large boneless chicken breasts (about 450 g/ 1 lb), cut into bite-sized pieces
2 large mangoes, chopped into cubes
salt, to taste
water, as needed
fresh coriander leaves, chopped, for garnish

Heat oil in a large non-stick wok, and sauté onions, chillies and ginger until lightly browned.

Add in turmeric, chilli and cumin and coriander powders, and fry for a few seconds before adding in the chicken pieces. Stir fry the chicken to coat well with spices, over a medium heat.

Add the mangoes, salt and a little water, and let the chicken cook, covered, for 8–10 minutes until done. If the curry starts to dry up, add in a bit more water and let it come to a boil.

Garnish with fresh coriander leaves.

Serves 4

coconut chicken curry

see variations page 109

You can often find this dish served at weddings or special occasions. Its wonderful flavour comes from blending aromatic spices with the creaminess of coconut milk.

2 tbsp light cooking oil
5–6 curry leaves, fresh or dried
1–2 dried red chillies
1 medium-sized onion, sliced
1 tbsp minced garlic
1 tsp coriander powder

1 tsp cumin powder
$^1/_4$ tsp turmeric powder
240 ml (8 fl oz) coconut milk
2 large boneless chicken breasts (about
    450 g/1 lb), cut into 2.5-cm (1-in) cubes
salt and pepper, to taste

Heat oil and sauté the curry leaves and dried chillies for a few seconds, until fragrant. Add in onions and garlic, and fry for several minutes, until onions turn tender and pink.

Mix in coriander and cumin and turmeric powders, and fry for a few seconds before adding the coconut milk. Allow the sauce to come to a boil, and then add chicken pieces, along with salt and pepper.

Cook, covered, for 10–12 minutes, until chicken is cooked through, adding water if necessary to get the consistency you like.

Serves 4

variations

chicken tikka masala

see base recipe page 87

paneer tikka masala

Prepare the basic recipe, substituting 280 g (10 oz) cubed paneer for the chicken. Reduce cooking time by 5 minutes.

mushroom tikka masala

Prepare the basic recipe, substituting 280 g (10 oz) button mushrooms for the chicken. Reduce cooking time by 5 minutes.

cauliflower tikka masala

Prepare the basic recipe, substituting 280 g (10 oz) cauliflower florets for the chicken. Reduce cooking time by 5 minutes.

lamb tikka masala

Prepare the basic recipe, substituting 450 g (1 lb) cubed boneless lamb for the chicken. Increase cooking time by 10 minutes, or until lamb is cooked through.

variations

home-style chicken curry

see base recipe page 88

chicken & potato curry

Prepare the basic recipe, adding in 2 medium-sized potatoes, peeled and
quartered, along with the chicken.

home-style veggie curry

Prepare the basic recipe, substituting 280 g (10 oz) chopped mixed vegetables
like carrots, peas, cauliflower, mushrooms and potatoes, for the chicken.

home-style egg curry

Prepare the basic recipe, substituting 6 hard-boiled eggs for the chicken.

home-style lamb curry

Prepare the basic recipe, substituting 450 g (1 lb) cubed boneless lamb for the
chicken. Increase cooking time by 10 minutes, or until lamb is cooked through.

variations

green chicken curry

see base recipe page 90

green egg curry
Prepare the basic recipe, substituting 6 hard-boiled eggs, cut in half, for the chicken. Reduce cooking time by 5 minutes.

green fish curry
Prepare the basic recipe, substituting 450 g (1 lb) cubed firm white fish for the chicken. Reduce cooking time by 5 minutes.

green prawn curry
Prepare the basic recipe, substituting 450 g (1 lb) peeled and deveined prawns for the chicken. Reduce cooking time by 5 minutes.

green aubergine curry
Cut 6–8 baby aubergines (with skin on) into 2.5-cm (1-in) pieces and sauté in light cooking oil until they are slightly brown along the edges. Prepare the basic recipe, substituting fried aubergine for the chicken. Reduce cooking time by 5 minutes.

green mushroom curry
Lightly sauté 350 g (12 oz) button mushrooms until slightly brown and moist. Prepare the basic recipe, substituting fried mushroom for chicken. Reduce cooking time by 5 minutes.

kadhai chicken

see base recipe page 93

kadhai paneer
Prepare the basic recipe, substituting 280 g (10 oz) cubed paneer for the chicken. Reduce cooking time by 5 minutes.

kadhai prawns
Prepare the basic recipe, substituting 450 g (1 lb) peeled and deveined prawns for the chicken. Reduce cooking time by 5 minutes.

kadhai mushroom
Prepare the basic recipe, substituting 280 g (10 oz) button mushrooms for the chicken. Reduce cooking time by 5 minutes.

kadhai fish
Prepare the basic recipe, substituting 450 g (1 lb) cubed firm white fish for the chicken. Reduce cooking time by 5 minutes.

kadhai potatoes
Prepare the basic recipe, substituting 340 g (12 oz) cubed potatoes for the chicken. Reduce cooking time by 5 minutes.

chicken & chickpea curry

see base recipe page 94

chickpea & potato curry
Prepare the basic recipe, substituting 340 g (12 oz) peeled cubed potatoes
for the chicken. Reduce cooking time by 5 minutes.

chicken & kidney bean curry
Prepare the basic recipe, substituting 170 g (6 oz) cooked red kidney beans
for the chickpeas. Reduce cooking time by 5 minutes.

chicken & spinach curry
Prepare the basic recipe, substituting 60 g (2 oz) well-rinsed chopped
spinach for chickpeas. Reduce cooking time by 5 minutes.

chickpea & paneer curry
Prepare the basic recipe, substituting 280 g (10 oz) cubed paneer for the
chicken. Reduce cooking time by 5 minutes.

chickpea & vegetable curry
Prepare the basic recipe, replacing chicken with 225 g (8 oz) each of diced
cauliflower and carrots. Reduce cooking time by 5 minutes.

chickpea & spinach curry
Prepare basic recipe, substituting 110 g (4 oz) chopped spinach for chicken.

chicken masala

see base recipe page 96

egg masala
Prepare the basic recipe, substituting 6 hard-boiled eggs for the chicken.
Reduce cooking time by 5 minutes.

prawn masala
Prepare the basic recipe, substituting 450 g (1 lb) peeled and deveined prawns
for the chicken. Reduce cooking time by 5 minutes.

fish masala
Prepare the basic recipe, substituting 450 g (1 lb) cubed firm white fish for the
chicken. Reduce cooking time by 5 minutes.

aubergine masala
Prepare the basic recipe, substituting 260 g (9 oz) chopped aubergine, skin on,
for the chicken. Cook as directed in main recipe.

kidney bean masala
Prepare the basic recipe, substituting 1 tin kidney beans for chicken.

potato masala
Prepare the basic recipe, substituting 340 g (12 oz) cubed potatoes for chicken.

variations

mango chicken curry

see base recipe page 99

mango prawn curry
Prepare the basic recipe, substituting 450 g (1 lb) peeled and deveined prawns for the chicken. Reduce cooking time by 5 minutes.

mango fish curry
Prepare the basic recipe, substituting 450 g (1 lb) cubed firm white fish for the chicken. Reduce cooking time by 5 minutes.

mango & pepper curry
Prepare the basic recipe, substituting 170 g (6 oz) each of seeded, chopped red and green peppers for the chicken. Reduce cooking time by 5 minutes.

variations

coconut chicken curry

see base recipe page 100

coconut fish curry
Prepare the basic recipe, substituting 450 g (1 lb) cubed firm white fish for the chicken. Reduce cooking time by 5 minutes.

coconut prawn curry
Prepare the basic recipe, substituting 450 g (1 lb) peeled and deveined prawns for the chicken. Reduce cooking time by 5 minutes.

coconut veggie curry
Prepare the basic recipe, substituting 340 g (10 oz) chopped mixed vegetables like carrots, potatoes and beans for the chicken. Reduce cooking time by 5 minutes.

coconut egg curry
Prepare the basic recipe, substituting 6 hard-boiled eggs, cut in half, for the chicken. Reduce cooking time by 5 minutes.

lamb

These tasty and aromatic lamb recipes are perfect
for a large weekend dinner shared with close family
and friends. Serve them alongside a spread of rice
and naans, and a huge salad.

keema matar

see variations page 124

Minced meat (*keema*) is a wonderful way to feed a large crowd on a low budget; combined with frozen peas (*matar*), this recipe is a definite winner at any picnic.

2 tbsp light cooking oil
1 tsp cumin seeds
1 cinnamon stick
1–2 dried bay leaves
2 whole black cardamom pods
1 large onion, finely chopped
450 g (1 lb) lean minced lamb

2 medium-sized tomatoes, finely chopped
$^1/_2$ tsp red chilli powder
1 tsp cumin powder
1 tsp coriander powder
$^1/_2$ tsp garam masala
140 g (5 oz) frozen peas, thawed
salt, to taste

Heat oil in a heavy saucepan and sauté cumin seeds and cinnamon, bay leaves and cardamom pods until they start to sizzle. Add in onions and lamb and fry until lightly browned.

Stir in tomatoes, chilli, cumin and coriander powders and garam masala, and cook until tomatoes soften and begin to pulp. Add in peas and salt, and cook, covered, for 15–20 minutes, until the meat is completely cooked through.

Serves 4

lamb & potato curry

see variations page 125

Lamb pairs wonderfully well with potatoes, and slow-cooking them together always produces great results.

2 tbsp light cooking oil
4–5 whole cloves
2 whole black cardamom pods
1 cinnamon stick
1 large onion, finely chopped
1 tbsp minced ginger
1 tbsp minced garlic
$1/2$ tsp chilli powder
1 tbsp coriander powder

1 tsp cumin powder
$1/2$ tsp garam masala
2 medium-sized tomatoes,
    finely chopped
900 g (2 lbs) lamb pieces, bone in
salt, to taste
water, as needed (about 475–700 ml)
2 medium-sized potatoes,
    peeled and quartered

Sauté whole cloves, cardamom and cinnamon with onions in hot oil until onions start to tenderise and are lightly browned. Add in ginger, garlic, chilli, coriander and cumin powders and garam masala, and fry for a few seconds.

Add in tomatoes and cook for a few minutes until they soften and pulp. Add lamb, salt and water to the consistency you like, and cook, covered, for about 40 minutes. Then add potatoes, and cook, covered, for another 20 minutes, until lamb is tender and potatoes are cooked through.

Serves 4

sesame lamb

see variations page 126

Lamb often requires plenty of time to cook, and it is best to let it simmer over a low heat. Make sure to check on it at regular intervals; prevent it from drying up by adding in a bit of water as needed.

450 g (1 lb) boneless lamb, sliced into 0.5-cm
   (1/4-in) strips
1 tbsp minced ginger
1 tbsp minced garlic
1/2 tsp red chilli powder
1/2 tsp black pepper powder
1 tsp coriander powder

2 tbsp light cooking oil
5–6 curry leaves, fresh or dried
1 small onion, thinly sliced
salt, to taste
water, as needed
1 tbsp white sesame seeds

Combine the ginger, garlic, chilli, black pepper and coriander powders, and rub the mixture on the lamb. Leave the meat to marinate for at least an hour in the fridge.

Heat oil in deep wok, and sauté the curry leaves and onions until lightly browned. Add in the lamb along with the marinade, and season with salt. Stir fry the lamb, adding water if necessary to keep it from sticking to the pan. Let the lamb cook, covered, for 20–25 minutes, until tender.

Mix in sesame seeds and serve.

Serves 4

pepper lamb

see variations page 127

In south India, curry leaves and black pepper are commonly used to flavour meat dishes. In this recipe, freshly ground black pepper adds a mild smokiness to the lamb, and the yoghurt gives it a slight tang.

2 tbsp light cooking oil
1 tsp cumin seeds
1 tsp coriander seeds
1 tsp fennel seeds
5 or 6 curry leaves, fresh or dried
1 medium-sized onion, thinly sliced
1 tbsp garlic, finely crushed
450 g (1 lb) lean boneless lamb, cubed

1 tbsp black pepper, freshly ground
140 g (5 oz) natural yoghurt, full fat or low fat, beaten until smooth
salt, to taste
fresh coriander leaves for garnish
water, as needed
lemon wedges

Heat oil in a heavy saucepan, and add cumin, coriander and fennel seeds, along with curry leaves, allowing them to sizzle.

Add in onions and garlic and sauté until lightly browned. Add in lamb, black pepper and yoghurt, and cook, covered, on a low heat for 25–30 minutes or until lamb is tender and cooked through, stirring occasionally and adding a little water if the food begins to stick to the bottom of the pan.

Season with salt and cook, covered, for another 5–10 minutes. Garnish with fresh coriander leaves. Serve with lemon wedges so diners can add a drizzle of lemon juice.

Serves 4

sweet & sour lamb

see variations page 128

Although this may appear to be a rich and heavy dish, it is simple enough to put together. Serve this at dinner parties to make your guests feel like you've slaved all day just for them.

1 tbsp minced ginger
1 tbsp minced garlic
$\frac{1}{2}$ tsp red chilli powder
$\frac{1}{2}$ tsp black pepper powder
1 tsp coriander powder
2 tbsp honey

salt, to taste
450 g (1 lb) boneless lamb, sliced into
    2.5-cm (1-in) short strips
2 tbsp light cooking oil for pan
2 tbsp fresh lemon juice

Mix together all the spices, including the honey and salt, and rub the mixture on the lamb; leave to sit for at least an hour in the fridge to marinate.

Add about 2 tablespoons of oil to a non-stick pan and cook the lamb along with the marinade over a medium heat, stirring occasionally, until cooked through.

Drizzle with fresh lemon juice and serve warm.

Serves 4

kofta curry

see variations page 129

Kofta are balls of minced meat. A great idea is to make an extra batch of the meatballs and freeze them, uncooked, so that you can bake them in the oven and serve them with mild chutney as appetisers on a later date.

450 g (1 lb) lean minced lamb
2 tbsp minced onion
2 tbsp fresh coriander leaves, finely chopped
1 tbsp breadcrumbs
$^1/_2$ tsp red chilli powder
$^1/_2$ tsp garam masala
salt, to taste
2 tbsp light cooking oil
1 large onion, finely chopped
1 tsp minced ginger

1 tsp minced garlic
2 medium-sized tomatoes, finely chopped
$^1/_2$ tsp cumin powder
1 tsp coriander powder
260 g (9 oz) natural yoghurt, full fat or low fat, beaten until smooth
salt, to taste
water, as needed

Mix the minced lamb with the onion, coriander leaves, breadcrumbs, chilli powder, garam masala and salt, and form into 24 tiny meatballs. Set aside.

Heat 2 tablespoons of oil in a heavy-bottomed deep pan and sauté onions, ginger and garlic until they start to brown and become tender. Add in tomatoes, cumin and coriander powders, yoghurt and salt, and let curry come to a boil.

Slowly add in meatballs and cook, covered, on a low heat for 15–20 minutes, until the meatballs are completely cooked. Add in water if the curry starts to dry and stick to the bottom of the pan.

Serves 4

lamb & spinach

see variations page 130

In India, this dish is traditionally served on cold winter nights when spinach and other leafy greens are in season and can be found in abundance in the markets.

2 tbsp light cooking oil
2 whole black cardamom pods
1 cinnamon stick
1 large onion, finely chopped
1 tbsp minced ginger
1 tbsp minced garlic
$^1/_2$ tsp chilli powder
1 tbsp coriander powder
1 tsp cumin powder

$^1/_2$ tsp garam masala
510 g (18 oz) natural yoghurt, full fat or low fat, beaten until smooth
900 g (2 lbs) leg or shoulder of lamb, bone-in, cut into 2.5-cm (1-in) cubes
water, as needed
60 g (2 oz) fresh spinach, finely chopped
salt, to taste

In a large pan, sauté cardamoms and cinnamon with onions in hot oil until onions start to soften and go brown. Add in ginger, garlic, chilli, coriander and cumin powders and garam masala, and fry for a few seconds.

Add in yoghurt and cook on a low heat for a few minutes, until well blended with the spices. Add lamb and a little water, and cook, covered, for about 40 minutes, still on a low heat. Add in spinach and salt, and cook, covered, for another 20 minutes until lamb is tender and completely cooked through.

Serves 4

bhuna lamb

see variations page 131

Because this curry is quite rich in flavour, you may want to serve it with something simple like naan or plain white rice to completely enjoy its robustness. *Bhuna* means to gently fry in oil to bring out the maximum flavour of the ingredients.

2 tbsp light cooking oil
1 tsp cumin seeds
1 large onion, sliced
900 g (2 lbs) boneless lamb, cut into 2.5-cm
    (1-in) cubes
2–3 green chillies, seeds included, finely
    chopped
1 tbsp minced ginger
1 tbsp minced garlic

$^1/_4$ tsp turmeric powder
$^1/_2$ tsp red chilli powder
$^1/_4$ tsp garam masala
1 tsp coriander powder
2 tbsp tomato paste
salt, to taste
water, as needed
fresh coriander leaves, finely chopped,
        for garnish

Heat oil in a pan and add cumin seeds. Once they start to sizzle, add in onions and fry until slightly browned.

Add in lamb, green chillies, ginger and garlic, and fry for a few minutes, until fragrant. Add in the turmeric, chilli powder, garam masala and coriander powder, and mix well. Once the meat starts to brown, add in the tomato paste and salt, and stir fry for a few minutes.

Add a little water and cover; cook on a low heat for 30–35 minutes, or until the meat is tender. Garnish with chopped coriander leaves.

Serves 4

variations

keema matar

see base recipe page 111

minced meat & potatoes
Prepare the basic recipe, adding in 170 g (6 oz) finely chopped potatoes along with the meat and omitting the peas.

minced meat & carrots
Prepare the basic recipe, adding in 140 g (5 oz) finely chopped carrots along with the meat, and omitting the peas.

minced meat & turnips
Prepare the basic recipe, adding in 140 g (5 oz) finely chopped white turnips along with the meat and omitting the peas.

minced meat & chickpeas
Prepare the basic recipe, adding in 170 g (6 oz) of cooked chickpeas along with the meat and omitting the peas. If tinned, rinse and drain the chickpeas and omit salt from the recipe.

variations

lamb & potato curry

see base recipe page 112

lamb & sweet potatoes
Prepare the basic recipe, substituting 280 g (10 oz) sweet potatoes for the regular potatoes.

lamb & pumpkin
Prepare the basic recipe, substituting 280 g (10 oz) chopped pumpkin for the potatoes.

lamb & apricots
Prepare the basic recipe, substituting 140 g (5 oz) dried apricots for the potatoes.

lamb & lentils
Prepare the basic recipe, substituting 400 g (14 oz) dried red lentils for the potatoes. Increase cooking time by 5 minutes, or until the lentils are soft.

variations

sesame lamb

see base recipe page 115

sesame chicken

Prepare the basic recipe, substituting 450 g (1 lb) cubed chicken breast for the lamb. Reduce cooking time by 5 minutes, or until the chicken is completely cooked through.

sesame mushrooms

Prepare the basic recipe, substituting 140 g (5 oz) baby mushrooms for the lamb. Reduce cooking time by 5 minutes.

sesame prawns

Prepare the basic recipe, substituting 450 g (1 lb) prawns, peeled and deveined, for the lamb. Reduce cooking time by 5 minutes.

sesame baby sweetcorn

Prepare the basic recipe, substituting 510 g (18 oz) tinned whole baby sweetcorn, rinsed and drained, for the lamb. Reduce cooking time by 5 minutes.

variations

pepper lamb

see base recipe page 116

pepper chicken
Prepare the basic recipe, substituting 450 g (1 lb) cubed chicken for the
lamb. Reduce cooking time by 5 minutes, or until the chicken is completely
cooked through.

pepper mushrooms
Prepare the basic recipe, substituting 280 g (10 oz) baby mushrooms for the
lamb. Reduce cooking time by 5 minutes.

pepper prawns
Prepare the basic recipe, substituting 450 g (1 lb) peeled, deveined prawns for
the lamb. Reduce cooking time by 5 minutes.

pepper baby sweetcorn
Prepare the basic recipe, substituting 510 g (18 oz) tinned whole baby
sweetcorn, rinsed and drained, for the lamb. Reduce cooking time by 5 minutes.

variations

sweet & sour lamb

see base recipe page 118

sweet & sour chicken
Prepare the basic recipe, substituting 450 g (1 lb) thinly sliced chicken for
the the lamb. Reduce cooking time by 5 minutes, or until the chicken is
completely cooked through.

sweet & sour mushrooms
Prepare the basic recipe, substituting 280 g (10 oz) baby mushrooms for the
lamb. Reduce cooking time by 5 minutes.

sweet & sour prawns
Prepare the basic recipe, substituting 450 g (1 lb) peeled, deveined prawns
for the lamb. Reduce cooking time by 5 minutes.

sweet & sour baby sweetcorn
Prepare the basic recipe, substituting 510 g (18 oz) whole tinned baby
sweetcorn for the lamb. Rinse and drain corn and omit salt from recipe.
Reduce cooking time by 5 minutes.

variations

kofta curry

see base recipe page 120

minty kofta curry
Prepare the basic recipe, adding in 2 tablespoons of minced fresh mint into the minced meat.

fennel kofta curry
Prepare the basic recipe, adding in 1 tablespoon of crushed fennel seeds into the minced meat.

ginger kofta curry
Prepare the basic recipe, increasing the minced ginger to 2 teaspoons.

chicken kofta curry
Prepare the basic recipe, substituting 450 g (1 lb) minced chicken for the minced lamb.

variations

lamb & spinach

see base recipe page 121

lamb & kasoori methi
Prepare the basic recipe, substituting 60 g (2 oz) chopped kasoori methi
(dried fenugreek leaves) for the spinach.

lamb & kale
Prepare the basic recipe, substituting 225 g (8 oz) chopped kale for
the spinach.

lamb & turnips
Prepare the basic recipe, substituting 280 g (10 oz) chopped white turnips
for the spinach.

lamb & beetroot
Prepare the basic recipe, substituting 280 g (10 oz) chopped beetroot for
the spinach.

lamb & carrots
Prepare the basic recipe, substituting 280 g (10 oz) chopped carrots for
the spinach.

variations

bhuna lamb

see base recipe page 123

bhuna lamb with peppers
Prepare the basic recipe, adding in 170 g (6 oz) cored, sliced peppers along with the tomato paste.

bhuna lamb with cabbage
Prepare the basic recipe, adding in 120 g (4 oz) chopped cabbage along with the tomato paste.

bhuna lamb with spinach
Prepare the basic recipe, adding in 30 g (1 oz) chopped fresh spinach, thoroughly rinsed, along with the tomato paste.

fish & prawns

Fish and prawns are extremely versatile and can

take on any flavour thrown at them with ease.

These recipes will have you hooked.

kerala fish curry

see variations page 148

The heat from the spices and the tartness of the tamarind in this dish will help the delicate flavours linger on your palate for a long time. It is from Kerala, on the southwest coast of India.

2 tbsp light cooking oil
1 tsp mustard seeds
7–8 curry leaves, fresh or dried
2–3 garlic cloves, sliced
1 medium onion, finely chopped
$\frac{1}{2}$ tsp red chilli powder
$\frac{1}{2}$ tsp coriander powder
$\frac{1}{4}$ tsp turmeric powder
1 tbsp tomato paste

1 tsp tamarind paste
2 medium tomatoes, finely chopped
2 large fillets (about 450 g/1 lb) of any firm
    white fish, cut into large chunks
water, as needed (about 240 ml/8 fl oz)
salt, to taste
fresh coriander leaves, finely chopped,
    to garnish

Heat oil in a deep pan and sauté mustard seeds and curry leaves until they start to sizzle. Add in garlic and onions, and fry until lightly browned.

Add in chilli, coriander and turmeric powders, tomato paste, tamarind and tomatoes, and cook until tomatoes start to soften and pulp. Slowly add in fish pieces, and stir to coat with the spices. Add in about 240 ml (8 fl oz) water or more, depending on the curry consistency you prefer, and let the curry simmer for 15–20 minutes, until the fish is cooked through.

Season with salt, and garnish with fresh coriander leaves.

Serves 4

ginger prawns

see variations page 149

This recipe is a breeze to make and is a definite crowd pleaser. Add it to your next party menu to treat your guests to a delicious surprise.

15–20 large prawns (about 900 g/2 lbs), peeled
    and deveined
1 tbsp ginger, finely chopped
$1/2$ tsp red chilli powder
$1/4$ tsp turmeric powder

1 tbsp tomato paste
2 tbsp fresh lemon juice
salt, to taste
3 tbsp light cooking oil
spring onion, finely chopped, for garnish

Marinate prawns with ginger, chilli powder, turmeric powder, tomato paste, lemon juice and salt, and set aside for 15 minutes.

Heat oil in a wide non-stick pan and fry prawns for 5–6 minutes, until lightly browned and crisp on both sides. Garnish with chopped spring onion.

Serves 4

prawn sambal

see variations page 150

A *sambal* is a chilli-based sauce or dish. Serve this curry on dosas, or with a side of plain basmati rice and some cool sliced cucumbers.

15–20 large prawns (about 900 g/2 lbs),
   peeled and deveined
1/4 tsp turmeric powder
1/2 tsp garlic powder
3 tbsp light cooking oil
2–3 garlic cloves, finely chopped
1 medium onion, finely sliced

1 large tomato, finely chopped
1 tbsp. tomato paste
1/2 tsp red chilli powder
1/2 tsp coriander powder
salt, to taste
instant dosas, to serve (see page 244)
fresh coriander leaves, to garnish

Marinate prawns with turmeric and garlic powders, and set aside for 15 minutes. Heat oil in a wide pan and fry prawns until lightly browned on both sides. Remove from pan and set aside.

In the same pan, sauté garlic and onions until soft and lightly browned. Add in tomatoes, tomato paste and chilli and coriander powders, and continue to fry, breaking up tomatoes until the mixture starts to dry out and give out oil.

Slowly slide in the fried prawns, and carefully mix them with the tomato mixture to coat. Keep heat low so nothing burns. Season with salt, allow to heat through for a few minutes, and serve warm, on instant dosas, garnished with fresh coriander.

Serves 4

coconut fish curry

see variations page 151

This curry comes from the southern part of India, an area that is abundantly rich in both coconuts and seafood.

2 tbsp light cooking oil
5–6 curry leaves, fresh or dried
2–3 garlic cloves, finely chopped
1 small onion, thinly sliced
$\frac{1}{4}$ tsp turmeric powder
$\frac{1}{2}$ tsp red chilli powder
$\frac{1}{4}$ tsp black pepper powder

$\frac{1}{2}$ tsp coriander powder
475 ml (16 oz) coconut milk
2 large fillets (about 450 g/1 lb) of any firm
   white fish, cut into bite-sized pieces
1 tsp kasoori methi
   (dried fenugreek leaves)
salt, to taste

Heat oil in a pan and sauté curry leaves and garlic until they start to sizzle. Add in onions and fry until lightly browned.

Add in turmeric, red chilli, black pepper and coriander powders, and sauté for a few seconds before adding the coconut milk. Allow mixture to come to a boil and then reduce heat; then add in fish pieces and kasoori methi. Season with salt, and cook, covered, for 10–12 minutes until the fish is cooked through. Check from time to time so you don't overcook the fish.

Serves 4

masala fried fish

see variations page 152

Serve this dish on a platter of fresh, crisp lettuce and thinly sliced onions. Sprinkle with some fresh lemon juice and serve with warm, crusty bread.

$1/2$ tsp red chilli powder
$1/2$ tsp garlic powder
1 tbsp coriander powder
1 tbsp cumin powder
$1/2$ tsp black pepper powder
$1/2$ tsp amchur powder

$1/4$ tsp turmeric powder
2 tbsp fresh lemon juice
salt, to taste
4 large fillets (about 450 g/1 lb)
   of any firm white fish
3–4 tbsp light cooking oil

Mix all the spices with the lemon juice and salt to form a smooth paste. Rub the spice paste all over the fish fillets and set aside in the fridge to marinate for 20–30 minutes.

Heat oil in a large frying pan, and shallow-fry the fish fillets on a medium heat for about 6–8 minutes on each side, until crisp and cooked through.

Serves 4

ginger & lime fish

see variations page 153

The spicy, tart flavours of this dish will awaken your senses and transport you to a whole new world of flavour mixing.

1 tbsp ginger, finely chopped
pinch of turmeric
1/4 tsp red chilli powder
1/4 tsp amchur powder
salt, to taste

2 tbsp fresh lime juice
2 large fillets (about 450 g/1 lb)
   of any firm white fish
1 tsp light cooking oil

Mix all the ingredients, except the fish, together. Rub the resulting paste on the fish fillets, and set aside in the fridge for 15–20 minutes to marinate.

Preheat oven to 175°C/Gas Mark 4 (350°F). Wrap each fillet tightly in foil, and bake for 15–20 minutes, until fish is cooked through.

Serves 4

prawn jalfrezi

see variations page 154

A *jalfrezi* is a type of curry in which marinated meat, fish or vegetables are fried in oil and spices to make a thick, dry dish. Since prawns tend to not have a strong flavour of their own, they are a perfect candidate to pair with the robustness of tomatoes, which makes them all the more succulent.

2 tbsp light cooking oil
1 tsp cumin seeds
1 tsp coriander seeds
1 tbsp thinly julienned pieces of fresh ginger
1 medium onion, sliced
1/4 tsp turmeric powder
1/2 tsp red chilli powder
1 tsp coriander powder
1/4 tsp amchur powder

1 tbsp tomato paste
15–20 large prawns (about 900 g/2 lbs), peeled and deveined
1 large tomato, cut into wedges
1 medium green pepper, seeded and sliced
salt, to taste
2 tbsp fresh coriander leaves, finely chopped, for garnish

Heat oil in a wide pan, and add in cumin and coriander seeds. Once they start to sizzle, add ginger and onions, and fry until the onions start to brown. Add turmeric, chilli, coriander and amchur powders, and sauté for a few seconds before adding the tomato paste.

Once the tomato paste starts to combine with the spices, add in prawns and stir fry to coat well with the spice paste; keep heat low so mixture does not burn.

Add in tomatoes, peppers, and salt, and cook, covered, for 5–10 minutes over a low heat, stirring occasionally, until prawns are cooked through. Garnish with coriander leaves and serve.

Serves 4

tamarind fish

see variations page 155

Serve this dish over a bowl of plain white rice, along with some chilled, sweet real lemonade to complement the tanginess.

2 tbsp light cooking oil
$1/2$ tsp mustard seeds
1 tsp garlic, finely chopped
1 medium onion, thinly sliced
$1/2$ tsp red chilli powder
$1/4$ tsp turmeric powder
1 medium tomato, finely chopped

1 tsp tamarind concentrate
2 large fillets (about 450 g/1 lb) of any firm
    white fish, cut into 2.5-cm (1-in) cubes
1 medium green pepper, seeded
    and thinly sliced
salt, to taste

Sauté mustard seeds, garlic and onions in hot oil until soft and lightly browned.

Add in chilli and turmeric powders, tomatoes and tamarind, and cook over a low heat until tomatoes pulp and blend in well with the spices.

Add in the fish and green peppers, and stir fry on a medium heat until the fish is cooked through, making sure it does not break up.

Serves 4

variations

kerala fish curry

see base recipe page 133

kerala prawn curry

Prepare the basic recipe, substituting 260 g (9 oz) shelled and deveined prawns for the fish.

kerala chicken curry

Prepare the basic recipe, substituting 260 g (9 oz) chopped boneless chicken for the fish. Increase cooking time by 10 minutes, or until chicken is completely cooked through.

mixed vegetable curry

Prepare the basic recipe, substituting 280 g (10 oz) chopped mixed vegetables like potatoes, carrots, cauliflower and peas for the fish. Adjust cooking time to ensure vegetables are completely cooked through.

kerala paneer curry

Prepare the basic recipe, substituting 450 g (1 lb) cubed paneer for the fish.

kerala egg curry

Prepare the basic recipe, substituting 4 hard-boiled eggs, halved, for the fish.

variations

ginger prawns

see base recipe page 134

garlic prawns
Prepare the basic recipe, substituting 1 tablespoon fresh chopped garlic for the ginger.

tamarind prawns
Prepare the basic recipe, substituting 1 teaspoon tamarind paste for the ginger.

lemony prawns
Prepare the basic recipe, substituting 1 tablespoon lemon zest for the ginger and omitting the tomato paste.

peppery prawns
Prepare the basic recipe, substituting 1 tablespoon crushed black peppercorns for the ginger and omitting the tomato paste.

fennel prawns
Prepare the basic recipe, substituting 1 tablespoon crushed fennel seeds for the ginger and omitting the tomato paste.

variations

prawn sambal

see base recipe page 137

fish sambal
Prepare the basic recipe, substituting 2 boneless fillets (about 450 g/1 lb) of any firm white fish, cut into cubes, for the prawns.

chicken sambal
Prepare the basic recipe, substituting 2 boneless chicken breasts (450 g/1 lb), cut into cubes, for the prawns. Increase cooking time by 10 minutes, or until chicken is completely cooked through.

potato sambal
Prepare the basic recipe, substituting 340 g (12 oz) cubed potatoes for the prawns. Increase cooking time by 10 minutes, or until potato is completely cooked through.

string bean sambal
Prepare the basic recipe, substituting 280 g (10 oz) green beans, cut into 2.5-cm (1-in) pieces, for the prawns.

baby sweetcorn sambal
Prepare the basic recipe, substituting 450 g (1 lb) chopped tinned baby sweetcorn, rinsed and drained, for the prawns.

variations

coconut fish curry

see base recipe page 138

coconut prawn curry

Prepare the basic recipe, substituting 260 g (9 oz) shelled and deveined prawns for the fish.

coconut egg curry

Prepare the basic recipe, substituting 6 hard-boiled eggs for the fish.

coconut chicken curry

Prepare the basic recipe, substituting 2 boneless chicken breasts (about 450 g/ 1 lb), cut into cubes, for the fish. Increase cooking time by 10 minutes, or until chicken is completely cooked through.

coconut potato curry

Prepare the basic recipe, substituting 340 g (12 oz) peeled, cubed potatoes for the fish. Increase cooking time by 10 minutes, or until potato is completely cooked through.

coconut chickpea curry

Prepare the basic recipe, substituting 85 g (3 oz) cooked chickpeas for the fish. If tinned, rinse and drain chickpeas and omit salt from recipe.

variations

masala fried fish

see base recipe page 140

minty fried fish
Prepare the basic recipe, adding in 1 tablespoon dried mint leaves along with the rest of the spices.

sesame fried fish
Prepare the basic recipe, adding in 1 tablespoon sesame seeds along with the rest of the spices.

fennel fried fish
Prepare the basic recipe, adding in 1 tablespoon crushed fennel seeds along with the rest of the spices.

lemony fried fish
Prepare the basic recipe, adding in 1 tablespoon lemon zest along with the rest of the spices.

curry leaf fried fish
Prepare the basic recipe, adding in 2 tablespoons dried crushed curry leaves along with the rest of the spices.

variations

ginger & lime fish

see base recipe page 143

garlic & lime fish
Prepare the basic recipe, substituting 1 tablespoon garlic for the ginger.

mint & lime fish
Prepare the basic recipe, substituting 1 tablespoon fresh mint for the ginger.

dill & lime fish
Prepare the basic recipe, substituting 1 tablespoon fresh dill for the ginger.

coriander & lime fish
Prepare the basic recipe, substituting 1 tablespoon fresh coriander leaves for
the ginger.

pepper & lime fish
Prepare the basic recipe, substituting 1 teaspoon crushed black peppercorns
for the ginger.

fennel & lime fish
Prepare the basic recipe, substituting 1 teaspoon crushed fennel seeds for
the ginger.

variations

prawn jalfrezi

see base recipe page 144

fish jalfrezi

Prepare the basic recipe, substituting 2 boneless fillets (about 450 g/1 lb) of any firm white fish, cut into cubes, for the prawns.

chicken jalfrezi

Prepare the basic recipe, substituting 2 boneless chicken breasts (about 450 g/ 1 lb), cut into cubes, for the prawns. Increase cooking time by 10 minutes, or until chicken is completely cooked through.

paneer jalfrezi

Prepare the basic recipe, substituting 280 g (10 oz) cubed paneer for the prawns.

mushroom jalfrezi

Prepare the basic recipe, substituting 170 g (6 oz) sliced mushrooms for the prawns.

potato jalfrezi

Prepare the basic recipe, substituting 340 g (12 oz) peeled, cubed potatoes for the prawns. Increase cooking time by 10 minutes, or until potato is completely cooked through.

tamarind fish

see base recipe page 147

tamarind prawns

Prepare the basic recipe, substituting 260 g (9 oz) shelled and deveined prawns for the fish.

tamarind chicken

Prepare the basic recipe, substituting 2 boneless chicken breasts (about 450 g/ 1 lb), cut into cubes, for the fish. Increase cooking time by 10 minutes, or until chicken is completely cooked through.

tamarind paneer

Prepare the basic recipe, substituting 280 g (10 oz) cubed paneer for the fish.

tamarind potatoes

Prepare the basic recipe, substituting 340 g (12 oz) cubed potatoes for the fish. Increase cooking time by 10 minutes, or until potato is completely cooked through.

tamarind eggs

Prepare the basic recipe, substituting 4 hard-boiled eggs, halved, for the fish.

paneer

Paneer is a soft mild cheese that is made by adding
lemon juice to hot milk in order to curdle it, and
then straining the mixture to get rid of any excess
moisture. Paneer is readily available at most ethnic
stores and can be bought in large blocks.

paneer-stuffed peppers

see variations page 167

These stuffed peppers make a delicious and easy midweek dinner, and they are perfect if you have vegetarian guests at a dinner party.

2 tbsp light cooking oil
1 tsp fennel seeds
1 tsp coriander seeds
450 g (1 lb) paneer, grated
$^1/_2$ tsp red chilli powder
$^1/_2$ tsp coriander powder

1 tsp cumin powder
1 tsp chaat masala
salt, to taste
4 small green peppers,
    halved lengthwise and cored
cooking oil spray for baking dish

Preheat oven to 175°C/Gas Mark 4 (350°F).

Heat oil in a non-stick saucepan and sauté fennel and coriander seeds until they start to sizzle.

Add in grated paneer and spices, and stir fry for a few minutes, until paneer is cooked through and well mixed with the spices. Season with salt.

Spray baking dish with cooking oil. Fill each pepper half with the paneer mixture and bake in the oven for 15–20 minutes, until the peppers have softened.

Serves 4

paneer & pea hash

see variations page 168

The mild flavour of paneer works perfectly paired with peas; combined with spices, this makes a wonderfully light and delicious curry.

2 tbsp light cooking oil
1 tsp cumin seeds
1 medium-sized onion, sliced
1 tsp minced garlic
$^{1}/_{2}$ tsp red chilli powder
$^{1}/_{4}$ tsp turmeric powder
$^{1}/_{2}$ tsp coriander powder

$^{1}/_{2}$ tsp garam masala
1 tbsp tomato paste
1 block paneer, about 450 g (1 lb), cut into bite-sized cubes
140 g (5 oz) frozen peas, thawed
salt, to taste

Heat oil in a non-stick wok and sauté cumin seeds, onions and garlic for a few minutes until lightly browned. Stir in chilli, turmeric and coriander powders, garam masala and tomato paste, and fry until fragrant.

Add in paneer and peas, season with salt, and stir fry for a few minutes until the paneer is cooked through and well coated with spices.

Serves 4

chilli paneer

see variations page 169

Since paneer is fairly quick to cook, it hardly takes any time to bring this dish together. To minimise the time you have to spend away from your dinner guests, you can keep all the ingredients prepped and ready to go.

2 tbsp cooking oil
1 tbsp minced ginger
1 tbsp minced garlic
1–2 green chillies, including seeds,
    finely chopped
1 medium-sized onion, finely chopped
450 g (1 lb) paneer, cut into
    2.5-cm (1-in) cubes

salt, to taste
$^1/_2$ tsp crushed black pepper
2 tbsp soy sauce
water, as needed
1 tbsp cornflour, mixed with 3 tbsp water
2 tbsp green onion, chopped, for garnish

In a non-stick pan, heat oil and sauté ginger, garlic and green chillies until fragrant. Add in onions and fry until lightly browned.

Add paneer pieces, salt, pepper and soy sauce, and cook for a minute. Add a splash of water and let mixture come to a boil, uncovered.

Pour in the cornflour mixture and stir until the sauce thickens, adding more water if necessary. Cover and cook for 2–3 minutes to allow paneer to absorb all the flavours, and garnish with chopped green onions.

Serves 4

potato & paneer curry

see variations page 170

As with most curries, leftovers of this dish will taste even better the next day, since the flavours will have had longer to blend in.

2 tbsp light cooking oil
1 tsp minced ginger
1 large onion, finely chopped
1 large tomato, finely chopped
1–2 green chillies, seeds included,
    finely chopped
1 tbsp tomato paste
$\frac{1}{2}$ tsp red chilli powder

$\frac{1}{4}$ tsp turmeric powder
1 tsp coriander powder
2 medium-sized potatoes, peeled and
    cut into bite-sized pieces
240 ml (8 fl oz) water
salt, to taste
450 g (1 lb) paneer, cut into bite-sized cubes

Sauté ginger and onions in hot oil until tender and lightly browned. Add in tomatoes, green chillies, tomato paste, chilli, and turmeric and coriander powders, and cook until tomatoes start to pulp and blend with the onions and spices.

Add in potatoes and water, season with salt, and cook, covered, for 10–15 minutes until potatoes are tender. Stir in paneer and cook for another 5–6 minutes until potatoes are completely cooked through.

Serves 4

south indian paneer

see variations page 171

On days when you're rushing to get dinner on the table, you can use this recipe as a filling for wraps or sandwiches, served with a big salad to complete the meal.

2 tbsp light cooking oil
1 tsp cumin seeds
1 tsp mustard seeds
5–6 curry leaves, fresh or dried
1 small onion, finely chopped
1 tbsp minced garlic
$^1/_4$ tsp turmeric powder

$^1/_2$ tsp red chilli powder
$^1/_2$ tsp coriander powder
450 g (1 lb) paneer, cut into 1.25-cm ($^1/_2$-in) cubes
140 g (5 oz) natural yoghurt, full fat or low fat, beaten until smooth
salt, to taste

Heat the cooking oil in a large frying pan. Add cumin and mustard seeds along with curry leaves and let them sizzle. Add in onions and garlic and fry until they start to soften. Mix in turmeric, chilli and coriander powders, and fry for a few seconds.

Stir in the paneer and yoghurt, season with salt, and cook for 6–8 minutes, or until the paneer is cooked through.

Serves 4

spicy scrambled paneer

see variations page 172

To bump up the nutritional value of this dish, throw in a handful of mixed frozen vegetables like carrots and peas along with the paneer, and cook until they get warmed through.

2 tbsp light cooking oil
1 tsp cumin seeds
1 tsp fennel seeds
1 tsp coriander seeds
1 small onion, finely chopped
1 tsp minced ginger
1 tsp minced garlic

450 g (1 lb) paneer, grated
$1/2$ tsp red chilli powder
$1/2$ tsp coriander powder
1 tsp cumin powder
1 tsp garam masala
1 small tomato, finely chopped
salt, to taste

Heat oil in a non-stick frying pan and sauté cumin, fennel and coriander seeds until they start to sizzle.

Add in onions, ginger and garlic, and fry until onions start to soften. Add in grated paneer, chilli, coriander and cumin powders and garam masala, and stir fry for a few minutes until the paneer is cooked through and coated with the spices.

Stir in tomatoes and cook for another 5–6 minutes, mixing well. Season with salt.

Serves 4

paneer butter masala

see variations page 173

This recipe is perfect for a week-night meal when you want comfort food with minimal effort.

2 tbsp light cooking oil
1 tsp cumin seeds
1 tsp minced ginger
$\frac{1}{2}$ tsp red chilli powder
1 tsp coriander powder
$\frac{1}{2}$ tsp garam masala

510 g (18 oz) pureed tomatoes (3 to 4 medium-sized tomatoes)
450 g (1 lb) paneer, cut into bite-sized pieces
2 tbsp cream
pinch of kasoori methi (dried fenugreek leaves)
salt, to taste

Sauté cumin seeds and ginger in hot oil until they start to sizzle. Add in chilli powder, coriander powder, garam masala and pureed tomatoes, and cook for a few minutes.

Stir in paneer, cream, kasoori methi and salt, and cook, covered, for 15–20 minutes until paneer is cooked through. Serve over rice, or with rotis.

Serves 4

variations

paneer-stuffed peppers

see base recipe page 157

potato-stuffed peppers
Prepare the basic recipe, substituting 340 g (12 oz) boiled potatoes for the paneer.

sweetcorn-stuffed peppers
Prepare the basic recipe, substituting 300 g (11 oz) thawed frozen sweetcorn for the paneer.

chicken-stuffed peppers
Prepare the basic recipe, substituting 225 g (8 oz) minced chicken for the paneer. Increase cooking time by 10 minutes, or until chicken is completely cooked through.

lamb-stuffed peppers
Prepare the basic recipe, substituting 225 g (8 oz) minced lamb for the paneer. Increase cooking time by 10 minutes, or until lamb is completely cooked through.

minty stuffed peppers
Prepare the basic recipe, adding in 1 tablespoon dried mint leaves along with the rest of the spices.

variations

paneer & pea hash

see base recipe page 158

potato & pea hash
Prepare the basic recipe, substituting 340 g (12 oz) peeled boiled potatoes for the paneer.

mushroom & pea hash
Prepare the basic recipe, substituting 140 g (5 oz) finely chopped mushrooms for the paneer.

carrot & pea hash
Prepare the basic recipe, substituting 225 g (8 oz) finely chopped carrots for the paneer.

cauliflower & pea hash
Prepare the basic recipe, substituting 140 g (5 oz) finely chopped cauliflower for the paneer.

chilli paneer

see base recipe page 160

chilli mushrooms
Prepare the basic recipe, substituting 140 g (5 oz) sliced mushrooms for
the paneer.

chilli cauliflower
Prepare the basic recipe, substituting 140 g (5 oz) chopped cauliflower for
the paneer.

chilli baby sweetcorn
Prepare the basic recipe, substituting 300 g (11 oz) tinned, chopped baby
sweetcorn, rinsed and drained well, for the paneer.

chilli potatoes
Prepare the basic recipe, substituting 300 g (11 oz) peeled, cubed boiled potatoes
for the paneer.

chilli prawns
Prepare the basic recipe, substituting 260 g (9 oz) peeled and deveined prawns
for the paneer.

variations

potato & paneer curry

see base recipe page 161

potato & pea curry
Prepare the basic recipe, substituting 300 g (11 oz) thawed frozen peas
for the paneer.

potato & cauliflower curry
Prepare the basic recipe, substituting 140 g (5 oz) chopped cauliflower for
the paneer.

potato & chickpea curry
Prepare the basic recipe, substituting 400 g (14 oz) cooked chickpeas for the
paneer. If tinned, rinse and drain chickpeas and omit salt from recipe.

potato & spinach curry
Prepare the basic recipe, substituting 60 g (2 oz) chopped spinach for
the paneer.

potato & egg curry
Prepare the basic recipe, substituting 4 hard-boiled eggs, cut in half, for
the paneer.

variations

south indian paneer

see base recipe page 162

south indian chicken
Prepare the basic recipe, substituting 450 g (1 lb) chicken breasts, chopped, for the paneer. Increase cooking time by 10 minutes, or until chicken is completely cooked through.

south indian mushrooms
Prepare the basic recipe, substituting 140 g (5 oz) baby mushrooms for the paneer. Increase cooking time by 10 minutes.

south indian prawns
Prepare the basic recipe, substituting 260 g (9 oz) peeled and deveined prawns for the paneer. Increase cooking time by 5 minutes, or until prawns are completely cooked through.

south indian baby sweetcorn
Prepare the basic recipe, substituting 300 g (11 oz) tinned, rinsed and drained baby sweetcorn for the paneer. Increase cooking time by 10 minutes.

variations

spicy scrambled paneer

see base recipe page 165

spicy scrambled eggs
Prepare the basic recipe, substituting 6 beaten eggs for the paneer.

spicy potato mash
Prepare the basic recipe, substituting 340 g (12 oz) boiled potatoes for the paneer.

spicy pea mash
Prepare the basic recipe, substituting 300 g (11 oz) thawed frozen peas for the paneer.

spicy sweetcorn mash
Prepare the basic recipe, substituting 300 g (11 oz) thawed frozen sweetcorn for the paneer.

variations

paneer butter masala

see base recipe page 166

butter chicken
Prepare the basic recipe, substituting 260 g (9 oz) chopped boneless chicken for
the paneer. Increase cooking time by 10 minutes, or until chicken is completely
cooked through.

butter mushrooms
Prepare the basic recipe, substituting 140 g (5 oz) chopped mushrooms for
the paneer.

butter prawns
Prepare the basic recipe, substituting 260 g (9 oz) peeled and deveined prawns
for the paneer.

butter cauliflower
Prepare the basic recipe, substituting 140 g (5 oz) chopped cauliflower for
the paneer.

vegetables

Indian cuisine is packed with fantastic vegetarian
recipes that are both healthy and delicious. These
dishes are wonderful as an accompaniment to a
main meal, but most also work perfectly as main
dishes themselves.

saag aloo

see variations page 196

Using frozen spinach makes this classic Indian dish a breeze to prepare; it comes together easily in no time. *Saag* is spinach and *aloo* are potatoes.

2 medium-sized potatoes, peeled,
    boiled and cut into 1.25-cm (½-in) cubes
light cooking oil for deep frying
1 tbsp minced garlic
1 tbsp light cooking oil
450 g (1 lb) frozen spinach,
    thawed and pureed

½ tsp red chilli powder
½ tsp coriander powder
½ tsp cumin powder
85 g (3 oz) natural yoghurt, full fat
    or low fat, beaten until smooth
salt, to taste

Deep-fry potatoes in light oil until brown on all sides. Set aside.

Sauté garlic in 1 tablespoon of hot oil until fragrant. Add in pureed spinach, chilli, coriander and cumin powders and yoghurt, and cook, covered, for 8–10 minutes until well blended.

Add in fried potatoes and salt, and cook, covered, for another 5–6 minutes.

Serves 4

aloo tamatar

see variations page 197

This traditional potato and tomato curry is often served on brunch menus along with deep-fried Indian bread called puris.

2 tbsp light cooking oil
1 tsp cumin seeds
1 medium-sized onion, finely chopped
$^1/_4$ tsp turmeric powder
$^1/_2$ tsp red chilli powder
$^1/_2$ tsp coriander powder

1 medium-sized tomato, finely chopped
2 medium-sized potatoes, peeled, boiled
    and cut into 1.25-cm ($^1/_2$-in) cubes
240 ml (8 fl oz) water
salt, to taste

Fry cumin seeds and onions in hot oil until onions starts to brown and become tender.

Add in turmeric, chilli and coriander powders and tomatoes, and cook for a couple of minutes until tomatoes start to pulp. Add in potatoes, water and salt, and cook, covered, for another 10–12 minutes.

Serves 4

mushroom masala

see variations page 198

Mushrooms are a great alternative to meat for most vegetarians, since they have a strong, meaty texture and can take on heavy flavours. This dish is a wonderful way to treat your vegetarian guests.

2 tbsp light cooking oil
1 tsp cumin seeds
1 medium-sized onion, finely chopped
10–12 baby mushrooms, including stems,
    quartered
1 tsp coriander powder
$^1/_4$ tsp turmeric powder

$^1/_2$ tsp red chilli powder
$^1/_2$ tsp garam masala
30 g (1 oz) natural yoghurt, full fat or low fat,
    beaten until smooth
120 ml (4 fl oz) water
salt, to taste

Fry cumin seeds and onions in hot oil, until they become tender. Add in mushrooms and fry for a couple of minutes until mixture starts to brown.

Add in coriander, turmeric and chilli powders, garam masala, yoghurt, water and salt, and cook, covered, for another 10–15 minutes.

Serves 4

spicy mashed potatoes

see variations page 199

This recipe is a perfect blend of East and West. It combines the classic dish of mashed potatoes from the Western world with the more traditional flavours of Indian cooking.

2 or 3 large potatoes, peeled, boiled
   and mashed
$1/2$ tsp cumin powder
$1/2$ tsp red chilli powder

$1/2$ tsp coriander powder
$1/2$ tsp amchur powder
salt, to taste

Mix mashed potatoes well with spices and salt. Serve warm.

Serves 4

sautéed beans

see variations page 200

You can serve this dish in warm tortillas with some fresh lettuce and tomatoes as a quick and simple wrap for lunch.

2 tbsp light cooking oil
1 tsp cumin seeds
225 g (8 oz) green beans, cut into
   2.5-cm (1-in) long pieces

$\frac{1}{4}$ tsp turmeric powder
$\frac{1}{2}$ tsp red chilli powder
1 tsp coriander powder
salt, to taste

Heat oil in a non-stick pan and sauté cumin seeds until they start to sizzle. Add in beans and turmeric, chilli and coriander powders, and stir fry for a few minutes.

Cook, covered, for 5–10 minutes, stirring occasionally, until beans become tender. Season with salt.

Serves 4

mixed-vegetable curry

see variations page 201

This dish is best enjoyed when served with a side of freshly made warm rotis and a light chutney. It also works well alongside a flavourful pulao and some salad.

2 tbsp light cooking oil
1 medium-sized onion, thinly sliced
$^1/_4$ tsp turmeric powder
$^1/_2$ tsp red chilli powder
1 tsp coriander powder
260 g (9 oz) mixed vegetables (peas, carrots,
    baby sweetcorn, mushrooms, mixed peppers)
    uncooked, chopped into small pieces

140 g (5 oz) potatoes, chopped (from about
    1 large potato)
1 large tomato, roughly chopped
2 tbsp natural yoghurt, low fat or full fat
salt, to taste
water, as needed
2 tbsp fresh coriander leaves, finely
    chopped, for garnish

Heat oil in a large pan and fry onions until they begin to soften. Add in turmeric, chilli and coriander powders and fry for a few seconds.

Add mixed vegetables and potatoes, and cook, covered, for 3–4 minutes. Add in tomatoes and cook for a few minutes until they begin to pulp.

Mix in yoghurt and salt, and stir curry until all ingredients are blended well. Add some water if the sauce becomes too dry and starts to stick. Cover and cook for 8–10 minutes, until potatoes are tender. Garnish with fresh coriander leaves.

Serves 4

baingan bharta

see variations page 202

Serve this flavourful dish alongside a simple dal and rice. *Baingan* means aubergines.

2 large aubergines (about 450 g/1 lb), unpeeled
2 tbsp light cooking oil, plus oil for
　roasting tin
1 tsp cumin seeds
2.5-cm (1-in) chunk of ginger, finely chopped
1 large onion, finely chopped

$^1/_4$ tsp turmeric powder
$^1/_2$ tsp red chilli powder
$^1/_4$ tsp garam masala
1 large tomato, finely chopped
salt, to taste
fresh coriander leaves, chopped, for garnish

Preheat oven to 200°C/Gas Mark 6 (400°F). Make tiny slits all around the aubergines, place them in an oiled roasting tin and roast in the oven for 30–35 minutes, until they get completely charred on the outside. Remove the charred skin and mash the pulpy insides of the aubergines. Set aside.

Heat 2 tablespoons oil in a pan and sauté cumin seeds and ginger until they start to sizzle. Add in onions and fry until lightly browned.

Add in turmeric, red chilli powder and garam masala, and fry for a few seconds until fragrant. Add in tomatoes and cook until pulpy.

Add the mashed aubergine and sauté for 10–15 minutes, stirring constantly to blend well. Add salt to taste. Garnish with coriander leaves.

Serves 4

aloo gobi

see variations page 203

A simple everyday Indian dinner usually includes a dal, rotis, some rice and a vegetable side, so it is quite common to find quick and simple vegetarian dishes like this being prepared. *Aloo* are potatoes and *gobi* is cauliflower.

2 tbsp light cooking oil
1 tsp cumin seeds
2 medium-sized potatoes, peeled and cubed
1 small cauliflower, cut into florets
$1/4$ tsp turmeric powder

$1/4$ tsp amchur powder
$1/2$ tsp red chilli powder
1 tsp coriander powder
salt, to taste

In a deep frying pan, sauté cumin seeds in hot oil until they start to sizzle. Add in potatoes and cauliflower, and fry for 15–20 minutes, stirring occasionally, until potatoes are tender. Mix in spices and salt, and stir fry for a few more minutes to blend well.

Serves 4

spiced carrots

see variations page 204

You can serve this dish as a side with some chicken or fish curry and a helping of rice. Throw in a salad, and you'll have a complete, well-balanced meal.

2 tbsp light cooking oil
1 tsp cumin seeds
2–3 large carrots, sliced
$\frac{1}{4}$ tsp turmeric powder

$\frac{1}{4}$ tsp amchur powder
$\frac{1}{2}$ tsp red chilli powder
salt, to taste

In a frying pan, sauté cumin seeds in hot oil until they start to sizzle. Add in carrots, turmeric, amchur powder and chilli powder, and fry for 15–20 minutes, stirring occasionally, until carrots are tender. Season with salt.

Serves 4

fried aubergine

see variations page 205

As you cook this dish, the spice blend penetrates through the aubergine, making it succulent on the inside and slightly crisp on the outside.

2 tbsp light cooking oil
1 large aubergine, peel on, sliced into
    1.25-cm ($\frac{1}{2}$-in) circles
$\frac{1}{4}$ tsp turmeric powder

$\frac{1}{4}$ tsp amchur powder
$\frac{1}{2}$ tsp red chilli powder
salt, to taste

Heat oil on a high heat in a wide non-stick pan and place aubergine slices in a single layer for 2–3 minutes on one side, until brown; then flip the slices and while the other sides cook for another 2–3 minutes, evenly sprinkle the tops with turmeric, amchur and chilli powders and salt.

Serves 4

dahi bhindi

see variations page 206

A quick, simple sauté of fresh okra (*bhindi*) in a blend of spices is a common, everyday dish, cooked in most Indian homes. Adding in yoghurt (*dahi*) takes this recipe to a whole new level.

2 tbsp light cooking oil
15–20 medium-sized okra, chopped
$^1/_4$ tsp turmeric powder
$^1/_2$ tsp red chilli powder
$^1/_2$ tsp coriander powder

$^1/_2$ tsp amchur powder
30 g (1 oz) natural yoghurt, full fat or low fat, beaten until smooth
salt, to taste

In a frying pan, fry the okra in hot oil until it starts to lightly brown. Add in all spices and stir fry for a few seconds.

Mix in yoghurt and salt and cook for 5–6 minutes, until the okra is completely cooked through.

Serves 4

dum aloo

see variations page 207

Dum is a way of steaming food in a pan with a tightly closed lid. You can serve this dish as a side with some dal and a flavoured pulao. It will also go well when paired with a light chicken curry and warm naans. Add a bowl of raita to complete the meal.

2 tbsp light cooking oil
8–10 baby red potatoes, peeled
$\frac{1}{2}$ tsp red chilli powder
$\frac{1}{4}$ tsp turmeric powder
1 tsp coriander powder
2 tbsp tomato paste
60 g (2 oz) natural yoghurt, full fat or low fat,
   beaten until smooth

water, as needed
salt, to taste
$\frac{1}{2}$ tsp kasoori methi
   (dried fenugreek leaves)
fresh coriander leaves,
   finely chopped, for garnish

Heat oil in a non-stick pan and sauté potatoes until lightly browned on all sides. Add in chilli, turmeric and coriander powders, and fry for a few seconds to coat potatoes well with spices.

Stir in tomato paste and yoghurt and cook over a medium heat, covered, for 10–15 minutes, until potatoes become tender. Add water if necessary to prevent the sauce sticking to the bottom of the pan.

Add in salt and kasoori methi, and cook for another 4–5 minutes. Garnish with fresh coriander leaves.

Serves 4

variations

saag aloo

see base recipe page 175

saag chicken
Prepare the basic recipe, substituting 260 g (9 oz) chopped boneless chicken for the potatoes. Increase cooking time by 10 minutes, or until the chicken is completely cooked through.

saag paneer
Prepare the basic recipe, substituting 260 g (9 oz) cubed paneer for the potatoes.

saag mushrooms
Prepare the basic recipe, substituting 140 g (5 oz) chopped mushrooms for the potatoes.

saag baby sweetcorn
Prepare the basic recipe, substituting 300 g (11 oz) chopped tinned baby sweetcorn, rinsed and drained well, for the potatoes.

variations

aloo tamatar

see base recipe page 176

aloo matar

Prepare the basic recipe, adding in 140 g (5 oz) thawed frozen peas along with the potatoes.

aloo gobi

Prepare the basic recipe, adding in 140 g (5 oz) chopped cauliflower along with the potatoes.

mushroom tamatar

Prepare the basic recipe, substituting 140 g (5 oz) chopped mushrooms for the potatoes.

prawn tamatar

Prepare the basic recipe, substituting 260 g (9 oz) peeled and deveined prawns for the potatoes.

variations

mushroom masala

see base recipe page 179

aubergine masala
Prepare the basic recipe, substituting 8 to 10 baby aubergines, cut into
quarters, for the mushrooms.

okra masala
Prepare the basic recipe, substituting 200 g (7 oz) chopped okra for
the mushrooms.

courgette masala
Prepare the basic recipe, substituting 140 g (5 oz) sliced courgette for
the mushrooms.

pepper masala
Prepare the basic recipe, substituting 260 g (9 oz) cored sliced red or green
peppers for the mushrooms.

spicy mashed potatoes

see base recipe page 180

mashed sweet potatoes
Prepare the basic recipe, substituting 340 g (12 oz) sweet potatoes for the potatoes.

mashed peas
Prepare the basic recipe, substituting 300 g (11 oz) thawed frozen peas for the potatoes.

mashed cauliflower
Prepare the basic recipe, substituting 140 g (5 oz) boiled cauliflower for the potatoes.

mashed carrots
Prepare the basic recipe, substituting 225 g (8 oz) boiled chopped carrots for the potatoes.

mashed turnips
Prepare the basic recipe, substituting 340 g (12 oz) boiled chopped white turnips for the potatoes.

mashed pumpkin
Prepare the basic recipe, substituting 400 g (14 oz) boiled chopped pumpkin for the potatoes.

variations

sautéed beans

see base recipe page 181

sautéed baby sweetcorn
Prepare the basic recipe, substituting 300 g (11 oz) tinned, chopped baby sweetcorn, rinsed and drained, for the green beans.

sautéed okra
Prepare the basic recipe, substituting 200 g (7 oz) chopped okra for the green beans.

sautéed courgette
Prepare the basic recipe, substituting 140 g (5 oz) sliced courgette for the green beans.

sautéed cabbage
Prepare the basic recipe, substituting 225 g (8 oz) chopped cabbage for the green beans.

sautéed peas
Prepare the basic recipe, substituting 300 g (11 oz) thawed frozen peas for the green beans.

mixed-vegetable curry

see base recipe page 182

spinach & sweetcorn curry

Prepare the basic recipe, substituting 140 g (5 oz) each of chopped spinach and frozen sweetcorn for the mixed vegetables.

cauliflower & pea curry

Prepare the basic recipe, substituting 140 g (5 oz) each of chopped cauliflower and frozen peas for the mixed vegetables.

carrot & pea curry

Prepare the basic recipe, substituting 140 g (5 oz) each of chopped carrots and frozen peas for the mixed vegetables.

variations

baingan bharta

see base recipe page 184

baingan bharta flatbread
Prepare the basic recipe. Spread a thin layer of the bharta on a garlic or plain naan or flatbread. Bake it in a 175°C/Gas Mark 4 (350°F) preheated oven for 8–10 minutes or until the naan begins to crisp. Sprinkle with chopped fresh mint leaves, cut into slices and serve warm.

bharta with peas
Prepare the basic recipe, adding in 140 g (5 oz) frozen peas along with the roasted aubergine.

aloo gobi

see base recipe page 187

gobi matar

Prepare the basic recipe, substituting 300 g (11 oz) frozen peas for the potatoes. Reduce cooking time by 5 minutes.

aloo matar

Prepare the basic recipe, substituting 300 g (11 oz) frozen peas for the cauliflower. Reduce cooking time by 5 minutes.

gobi gajar

Prepare the basic recipe, substituting 2 large carrots, chopped, for the potatoes.

variations

spiced carrots

see base recipe page 188

spiced cabbage
Prepare the basic recipe, substituting 225 g (8 oz) chopped cabbage for carrots.

spiced baby sweetcorn
Prepare the basic recipe, substituting 300 g (11 oz) tinned chopped baby sweetcorn, rinsed and drained, for the carrots.

spiced beetroot
Prepare the basic recipe, substituting 280 g (10 oz) sliced beetroot for carrots.

spiced radishes
Prepare the basic recipe, substituting 225 g (8 oz) sliced radishes for carrots.

spiced peppers
Prepare the basic recipe, substituting 260 g (9 oz) cored, sliced peppers for the carrots.

spiced spinach
Prepare the basic recipe, substituting 120 g (4 oz) well rinsed, chopped spinach for the carrots.

fried aubergine

see base recipe page 190

fried potatoes
Prepare the basic recipe, substituting 2 large peeled potatoes, cut in rounds, for the aubergine.

fried courgette
Prepare the basic recipe, substituting 2 large courgettes, cut in rounds 1.25 cm (½ in) wide, for the aubergine.

fried mushrooms
Prepare the basic recipe, substituting 8 portobello mushrooms, stems removed, caps left whole, for the aubergine.

fried carrots
Prepare the basic recipe, substituting 2 large carrots, cut in rounds, for the aubergine.

variations

dahi bhindi

see base recipe page 193

dahi aubergine
Prepare the basic recipe, substituting 140 g (5 oz) chopped aubergine for okra.

dahi courgette
Prepare the basic recipe, substituting 140 g (5 oz) chopped courgette for okra.

dahi baby sweetcorn
Prepare the basic recipe, substituting 300 g (11 oz) tinned chopped baby sweetcorn, rinsed and drained, for okra.

dahi green beans
Prepare the basic recipe, substituting 300 g (11 oz) chopped green beans for okra.

dahi mushrooms
Prepare the basic recipe, substituting 140 g (5 oz) chopped mushrooms for okra.

dahi peppers
Prepare the basic recipe, substituting 260 g (9 oz) cored, chopped peppers for okra.

variations

dum aloo

see base recipe page 194

dum aloo with mint
Prepare the basic recipe. Once the potatoes are cooked, mix in 3 tablespoons chopped fresh mint.

dum aloo with peas
Prepare the basic recipe, adding in 300 g (11 oz) frozen peas along with the potatoes.

dum aloo with raisins
Prepare the basic recipe, adding in 85 g (3 oz) raisins along with the potatoes.

pulses

Many traditional Indian dishes are based around beans and lentils, known as dal. Give these hearty recipes a try the next time you want something simple, yet delicious and satisfying.

dal tadka

see variations page 217

As they are chock-full of protein, lentils are a great addition to a vegetarian diet. They can easily take on varied flavours and add richness to your daily meals.

140 g (5 oz) dried red lentils, washed
   and drained
500 ml (17 fl oz) water
1 small onion, finely chopped
1 small tomato, finely chopped
1–2 green chillies, including seeds, chopped
2 garlic cloves, slit halfway through the middle
$^1/_4$ tsp turmeric powder

$^1/_4$ tsp red chilli powder
1 tsp cumin seeds
1 tsp fennel seeds
2 tbsp light cooking oil
salt, to taste
fresh coriander leaves, finely chopped,
   for garnish

Put the lentils, water, onions, tomatoes, chillies, garlic, turmeric powder and chilli powder into a large, heavy-bottomed pan, and cook on the hob on a low heat until lentils start to soften and pulp. Set aside.

In a small frying pan, fry cumin and fennel seeds in oil, until they start to sizzle and lightly brown. Be very careful not to burn them. Stir the fried cumin and fennel, together with the oil, into the cooked dal.

Season with salt and garnish with fresh coriander leaves.

Serves 4

mixed dal

see variations page 218

In many Indian households, a different dal (using varieties of dried beans, peas and lentils) is cooked each day, accompanied by a complementing vegetable.

2 tbsp light cooking oil
1 tsp cumin seeds
1 tsp fennel seeds
1 small onion, thinly sliced
1 medium tomato, chopped
1 tsp ginger, finely chopped
1 tsp garlic, finely chopped
1/4 tsp turmeric powder
1/2 tsp red chilli powder

1/2 tsp coriander powder
85 g (3 oz) dry red lentils, washed
    and drained
85 g (3 oz) dry split pea lentils, washed
    and drained
85 g (3 oz) dry green mung beans, washed
    and drained
500 ml (17 fl oz) water
salt, to taste

Heat oil in an open pressure cooker and fry cumin and fennel seeds until they start to sizzle. Add in onions and fry until they are lightly browned.

Add in tomatoes, ginger, garlic and turmeric, chilli and coriander powders, and fry until tomatoes start to soften. Add in red lentils, split pea lentils and mung beans, and sauté for a few seconds. Pour in water, and, once it boils, close pressure cooker and cook for 15–20 minutes, so lentils soften and completely cook through. Season with salt.

Serves 4

sambhar

see variations page 219

If you plan to serve this at a dinner party, pair it with a rich chicken or lamb curry, a flavourful pulao, a dry vegetable side dish, and some raita or salad on the side.

2 tbsp light cooking oil
1 tsp cumin seeds
1 tsp mustard seeds
6–7 curry leaves, fresh or dried
2–3 garlic cloves, sliced
1 medium onion, finely chopped
1/4 tsp turmeric powder
1/2 tsp red chilli powder
1 tsp sambhar powder

1 medium tomato, finely chopped
1 tsp tamarind concentrate
85 g (3 oz) dried yellow lentils, washed
   and drained
600 ml (20 fl oz) water
salt, to taste
squeeze of fresh lemon juice
fresh coriander leaves, finely chopped,
   for garnish

Heat oil in an open pressure cooker and sauté cumin and mustard seeds and curry leaves until they start to sizzle. Add in garlic and onions, and fry until soft and lightly browned. Add in turmeric, chilli and sambhar powders, and sauté for a few seconds before adding tomatoes and tamarind. Let the tomatoes cook until they pulp, with the cooker still open, and then add in lentils, water and salt. Let the mixture come to the boil, and then close the pressure cooker and cook for 20–25 minutes, by which time the lentils should be soft and mushy. If not, a few more minutes of pressure cooking might be required.

After opening the cooker, add in a bit more water to thin down the sauce if you wish, depending on desired consistency. Season with fresh lemon juice and garnish with fresh coriander leaves.

Serves 4

rajma

see variations page 220

Rajma are red kidney beans. Turn this dish into a one-pan meal by serving it alongside some crusty bread for dipping.

2 tbsp light cooking oil
1 tsp cumin seeds
1 medium onion, finely chopped
1 tsp ginger–garlic paste
2 medium tomatoes, finely chopped
1 tbsp tomato paste
$\frac{1}{2}$ tsp red chilli powder
$\frac{1}{2}$ tsp coriander powder

$\frac{1}{4}$ tsp garam masala
85 g (3 oz) cooked red kidney beans, fresh or
    tinned, rinsed and drained
water, about 240 ml (8 fl oz), as needed
salt, to taste
fresh coriander leaves, finely chopped,
    for garnish

Heat oil in large pan and sauté cumin seeds until they start to sizzle. Add in onions and fry until they soften. Add in ginger–garlic paste, tomatoes, tomato paste, chilli powder, coriander powder and garam masala, and fry until tomatoes pulp and the mixture starts to leave oil around the sides of the pan.

Add in kidney beans and about 240 ml (8 fl oz) of water, and let the sauce come to a boil. Lower the heat, and simmer for 10–15 minutes to allow the flavours to blend in. You can add in more water if you prefer a thinner curry.

Season with salt and garnish with fresh coriander leaves.

Serves 4

chana masala

see variations page 221

This robust dish is best enjoyed with a side of plain rice or warm, oven-fresh naans.

2 tbsp light cooking oil
1 tsp cumin seeds
1 medium onion, finely chopped
1–2 hot green chillies, including seeds, chopped
1 tsp ginger–garlic paste
2 medium tomatoes, finely chopped
1 tbsp tomato paste
$^{1}/_{2}$ tsp red chilli powder
$^{1}/_{2}$ tsp coriander powder
$^{1}/_{2}$ tsp cumin powder

$^{1}/_{4}$ tsp turmeric powder
$^{1}/_{4}$ tsp amchur powder
$^{1}/_{4}$ tsp garam masala
260 g (9 oz) cooked chickpeas (chana), fresh
    or tinned, rinsed and drained
water, about 240 ml (8 fl oz), as needed
salt, to taste
fresh coriander leaves, finely chopped,
    for garnish

Heat oil in large pan and sauté cumin seeds until they start to sizzle. Add in onions and chillies, and fry until onions soften. Add in ginger–garlic paste, tomatoes, tomato paste and remaining spices, and fry until tomatoes pulp and the mixture starts to leave oil around the sides of the pan.

Add in chickpeas and about 240 ml (8 fl oz) of water, and allow the curry come to a boil. Lower the heat, and simmer for 10–15 minutes to allow the flavours to blend in. You can add in more water if you prefer a thinner curry. Season with salt and garnish with fresh coriander leaves.

Serves 4

variations

dal tadka

see base recipe page 209

spinach dal

Prepare the basic recipe, adding in 60 g (2 oz) well-rinsed chopped fresh spinach along with the lentils.

fenugreek dal

Prepare the basic recipe, adding in 60 g (2 oz) chopped fresh fenugreek leaves along with the lentils.

carrot dal

Prepare the basic recipe, adding in 225 g (8 oz) chopped carrots along with the lentils.

cauliflower dal

Prepare the basic recipe, adding in 140 g (5 oz) chopped cauliflower along with the lentils.

courgette dal

Prepare the basic recipe, adding in 140 g (5 oz) chopped courgette along with the lentils.

variations

mixed dal

see base recipe page 210

mixed dal with lemon & mint

Prepare the basic recipe. Once the dal is cooked, mix in 3 tablespoons minced fresh mint and 2 tablespoons fresh lemon juice.

mixed dal with tamarind

Prepare the basic recipe, adding in 1 tablespoon tamarind paste along with the tomatoes.

mixed dal with peas & carrots

Prepare the basic recipe, adding in 140 g (5 oz) frozen peas and carrots along with the tomatoes.

variations

sambhar

see base recipe page 213

spinach sambhar
Prepare the basic recipe, adding in 60 g (2 oz) well-rinsed chopped spinach along with the lentils.

fenugreek sambhar
Prepare the basic recipe, adding in 60 g (2 oz) chopped fresh fenugreek leaves along with the lentils.

carrot sambhar
Prepare the basic recipe, adding in 225 g (8 oz) chopped carrots along with the lentils.

cauliflower sambhar
Prepare the basic recipe, adding in 140 g (5 oz) chopped cauliflower along with the lentils.

courgette sambhar
Prepare the basic recipe, adding in 140 g (5 oz) chopped courgette along with the lentils.

variations

rajma

see base recipe page 214

rajma with mint
Prepare the basic recipe, mixing in 2 tablespoons chopped fresh mint once the kidney beans are cooked.

rajma with dill
Prepare the basic recipe, mixing in 2 tablespoons chopped fresh dill once the kidney beans are cooked.

rajma with fennel
Prepare the basic recipe, mixing in 1 tablespoon dry-roasted, crushed fennel seeds once the kidney beans are cooked.

variations

chana masala

see base recipe page 216

chana masala with potatoes
Prepare the basic recipe, adding in 2 medium-sized potatoes, cubed, along with
the tomatoes. Increase cooking time by 10 minutes, or until potatoes are
tender and cooked through.

chana masala with mint
Prepare the basic recipe, mixing in 2 tablespoons minced fresh mint once the
chickpeas are cooked.

rajma masala
Prepare the basic recipe, substituting white kidney beans for the chickpeas.

side dishes

Don't let a fantastic curry down by just serving it with plain rice – these delicious, tasty sides will complement the main dish, complete the meal and create a wonderful spread.

pea pulao

see variations page 245

When hosting a dinner party, you can make this pulao a day ahead, since it keeps well and the flavours will infuse more richly. Just heat it in a microwave right before serving and fluff out the rice with a fork to prevent breaking the grains.

2 tbsp light cooking oil
1 tsp cumin seeds
1 cinnamon stick
3–4 cloves
1 bay leaf

1 small onion, thinly sliced
520 ml (18 fl oz) water
salt, to taste
260 g (9 oz) basmati rice, washed and rinsed
1 cup frozen peas, thawed

Heat oil in a deep non-stick pan. Add in cumin seeds, cinnamon, cloves and a bay leaf, and fry for a few seconds. Add in onions and continue to fry until they start to lightly brown.

Add in water, salt and rice, and cook on a medium-low heat, covered, until all the water is absorbed and the rice is tender.

Add in peas and cook for another 5 minutes, covered, on a low heat. Gently fluff the rice with a fork to mix the peas through.

Serves 4

mixed-bean salad

see variations page 246

Replace your everyday salad with this healthy and delightful version.

400 g (14 oz) of a variety of beans, cooked,
    rinsed thoroughly and drained (choose from
    kidney beans, chickpeas, black beans, pinto
    beans and cannellini and cook at home)
1 small onion, finely chopped
1 small tomato, finely chopped
85 g (3 oz) cucumber, finely chopped
$1/4$ tsp red chilli powder

2 tbsp fresh coriander leaves,
    finely chopped
$1/4$ tsp cumin powder
$1/2$ tsp garlic powder
$1/4$ tsp chaat masala
1 tbsp olive oil
1 tbsp fresh lemon juice
salt and pepper, to taste

Mix all the ingredients in a bowl and let the salad rest in the fridge for 15–20 minutes.
Serve chilled.

Serves 4

sprout salad

see variations page 247

You could serve this either as a first course or alongside a spicy meat curry. For a quick fix, I also like to add in a few extra veggies, like tomatoes, and turn it into a nice, filling lunch or light dinner.

260 g (9 oz) mung bean sprouts,
   rinsed thoroughly
1 small onion, finely chopped
85 g (3 oz) frozen sweetcorn, thawed
2 tbsp fresh coriander leaves, finely chopped

$1/4$ tsp red chilli powder
$1/4$ tsp garlic powder
$1/2$ tsp chaat masala
1–2 tbsp fresh lemon juice
salt, to taste

Mix all the ingredients in a bowl and leave the salad to rest in the fridge for 15–20 minutes. Serve chilled.

Serves 4

spiced potato salad

see variations page 248

The dish literally takes minutes to bring together, but what I've realised with time is that if you let it sit for a short time, the flavours intensify.

10–12 baby potatoes, skin on,
 boiled and halved
2 tbsp fresh coriander leaves,
 finely chopped
2 tbsp olive oil
1/4 tsp red chilli powder

1/4 tsp coriander powder
1/4 tsp cumin powder
1/2 tsp garlic powder
1/2 tsp chaat masala
2 tbsp fresh lemon juice
salt and pepper, to taste

Mix all the ingredients in a bowl and leave the salad to rest in the fridge for 15–20 minutes before serving.

Serves 4

masala slaw

see variations page 249

Coleslaw is generally packed with mayonnaise, and this makes it a forbidden dish for diet-conscious eaters. By replacing the mayo with yoghurt and adding in a pinch of Indian spices, you can now eat as much as you want!

260 g (9 oz) shredded green cabbage
30 g (1 oz) shredded purple cabbage
30 g (1 oz) shredded carrots
  (about 1 large carrot)
2 tbsp fresh coriander leaves,
  finely chopped
1 tbsp fresh mint leaves,
  finely chopped

140 g (5 oz) natural yoghurt, full fat or
  low fat, beaten until smooth
$\frac{1}{2}$ tsp red chilli powder
$\frac{1}{4}$ tsp cumin powder
$\frac{1}{2}$ tsp garlic powder
1 tbsp fresh lemon juice
salt and pepper, to taste

Mix all the ingredients in a bowl and let the slaw rest in the fridge for 15–20 minutes. Serve chilled.

Serves 4

chickpea & onion salad

see variations page 250

Boiled chickpeas mixed with onions, chillies, spices and a mix of chutneys are usually enjoyed as a quick snack sold by street vendors in northern India. Here is a quick, delicious, home version.

400 g (14 oz) cooked chickpeas, fresh
   or tinned, thoroughly rinsed
1 small onion, finely chopped
2 tbsp fresh coriander leaves,
   finely chopped
1/4 tsp red chilli powder

1/4 tsp cumin powder
1/4 tsp garlic powder
1/2 tsp chaat masala
1 tbsp fresh lemon juice
salt, to taste

Mix all the ingredients in a bowl and let the salad rest in the fridge for 15–20 minutes before serving.

Serves 4

cumin rice

see variations page 251

This side is best served with a rich curry or a heavy lentil dish. The cumin adds a delicate trail of sweetness to the dish and will leave your kitchen smelling heavenly.

2 tbsp light cooking oil
1 tbsp cumin seeds
1 bay leaf

520 ml (18 fl oz) water
salt, to taste
260 g (9 oz) basmati rice, washed and rinsed

Heat oil in a deep non-stick pan. Add in cumin seeds and fry for a few seconds until they start to sizzle. Add in a bay leaf, water, salt and rice, and cook on a medium-low heat, covered, until all the water is absorbed and the rice is tender.

Serves 4

coriander & mint rice

see variations page 252

You can vary this recipe seasonally, depending on what herbs are available in shops at
the given time. The flavour and texture of the dish will change, but it will be worth the
effort every time.

520 ml (18 fl oz) water
260 g (9 oz) basmati rice,
    washed and rinsed
85 g (3 oz) fresh coriander leaves,
    finely chopped

85 g (3 oz) fresh mint leaves,
    finely chopped
2 tbsp fresh lemon juice
salt, to taste

Bring the water to the boil before adding rice, and cook, covered, until all the water
evaporates. Let the rice cool to room temperature.

Gently fluff the rice with a fork and slowly mix in coriander, mint and lemon juice. Season
with salt.

Serves 4

cranberry & raisin pulao

see variations page 253

Serve this rice dish alongside an array of kebabs or grilled chicken. It also works well by itself, with a dollop of chutney, as it is traditionally served.

2 tbsp light cooking oil
1 cinnamon stick
3–4 cloves
1 bay leaf
1 small onion, thinly sliced

30 g (1 oz) dried cranberries
30 g (1 oz) raisins
520 ml (18 fl oz) water
salt, to taste
260 g (9 oz) basmati rice, washed and rinsed

Heat oil in a deep non-stick pan. Add in cinnamon, cloves and a bay leaf, and fry for a few seconds. Add in onions and fry until they start to lightly brown. Add in cranberries and raisins, and continue to fry for a minute so that they plump.

Add water, salt and rice, and cook on a medium-low heat, covered, until all the water evaporates and the rice is tender.

Serves 4

tomato rice

see variations page 254

Make this dish at the peak of summer, when tomatoes are at their best.

1 tbsp light cooking oil
1 tsp mustard seeds
6–7 curry leaves, fresh or dried
2 garlic cloves, sliced
1 medium onion, sliced thinly
$\frac{1}{4}$ tsp turmeric powder

$\frac{1}{4}$ tsp red chilli powder
1 medium tomato, chopped
salt, to taste
140 g (5 oz) cooked white basmati rice
fresh coriander leaves, finely chopped,
    to garnish

Heat oil in a non-stick pan and add mustard seeds, curry leaves and garlic. When they start to sizzle, add in sliced onions.

Once the onions start to lightly brown, add turmeric, chilli powder, tomatoes and salt. Cook for a few minutes until tomatoes begin to pulp.

Add in cooked rice and stir fry until well mixed with all spices. Garnish with chopped coriander leaves and serve warm.

Serves 4

chicken pulao

see variations page 255

Pairing meat and rice in a one-pan meal is a great way to feed a big group. Top that with some aromatic spice and a handful of fresh herbs, and you've got a definite crowd pleaser. Chicken pulao can also be a main dish.

2 tbsp light cooking oil
1 tsp cumin seeds
1 tsp coriander seeds
1 cinnamon stick
3–4 cloves
7–8 black peppercorns
1 bay leaf
1 small onion, thinly sliced
1 tsp ginger, finely chopped
1 tsp garlic, finely chopped

2 chicken breasts (about 450 g/1 lb) cut into
    2.5-cm (1-in) pieces
$\frac{1}{2}$ tsp red chilli powder
$\frac{1}{2}$ tsp coriander powder
$\frac{1}{2}$ tsp garam masala
$\frac{1}{2}$ tsp dried mint
520 ml (18 fl oz) water
salt, to taste
260 g (9 oz) basmati rice, washed and rinsed
fresh coriander leaves, finely chopped,
    to garnish

Heat oil in a deep non-stick pan. Add in cumin seeds, coriander seeds, cinnamon, cloves, peppercorns and bay leaf, and fry for a few seconds. Add in onions, ginger and garlic, and fry until mixture starts to lightly brown.

Add in chicken and chilli powder, coriander powder, garam masala and mint, and fry until the chicken turns opaque, stirring continuously with a spoon. Add in water, salt and rice, and cook on a medium-low heat, covered, until the water has been absorbed and the rice is tender.

Garnish with fresh coriander leaves.
Serves 4

besan chila

see variations page 256

These Indianised crepes are traditionally served as a light evening snack with chutneys. However, you can also serve them during brunch as a change from the regular sweetened versions.

260 g (9 oz) chickpea flour (besan)
$^1/_2$ tsp fennel seeds
$^1/_4$ tsp red chilli powder
$^1/_4$ tsp garlic powder
2 tbsp fresh coriander leaves,
    finely chopped

salt, to taste
water as needed
light cooking oil, as needed

Mix together the chickpea flour, spices, coriander leaves and salt. Add enough water to create a thin batter. Stir well.

Heat a few drops of oil in a non-stick pan, and pour in a ladleful of batter. Swirl the pan around to allow the batter to spread evenly, and fry on one side; turn pancake and fry until both sides are slightly crisp and pancake is cooked through, adding more oil if necessary while frying.

Serves 4

instant dosa

see variations page 257

A dosa is a crepe or pancake made from a batter of rice flour and ground pulses (peas, beans or lentils). In instant dosa flour, all the ingredients are already prepared and assembled, so the rest is easy. Serve these with a variety of chutneys or a light curry for a simple and delicious dinner. Any leftovers keep really well, and are great for lunch the next day.

260 g (9 oz) instant dosa flour
¼ tsp red chilli powder
30 g (1 oz) grated carrots
2 tbsp fresh coriander leaves, finely chopped
salt, to taste

water, as needed
light cooking oil, as needed

In a bowl, mix the dosa flour with chilli powder, carrots, coriander leaves and salt, and add in water slowly to form a smooth, thin crepe-like batter.

Heat a few drops of oil in a non-stick pan, and pour in a ladleful of batter. Swirl the pan to allow the batter to spread evenly, and fry on one side; turn and fry until both sides are slightly crisp, adding in more oil while frying if necessary.

Serves 4

pea pulao

see base recipe page 223

carrot pulao

Prepare the basic recipe, substituting 140 g (5 oz) finely chopped carrots for the peas.

sweetcorn pulao

Prepare the basic recipe, substituting 140 g (5 oz) thawed frozen sweetcorn for the peas.

courgette pulao

Prepare the basic recipe, adding in 140 g (5 oz) finely chopped courgette along with the onions. Omit the peas.

tomato pulao

Prepare the basic recipe, adding in 140 g (5 oz) finely chopped tomatoes along with the onions. Omit the peas.

chickpea pulao

Prepare the basic recipe, adding in 140 g (5 oz) cooked chickpeas along with the onions. If using tinned chickpeas, rinse and drain. Omit the peas.

pepper pulao

Prepare the basic recipe, adding in 140 g (5 oz) cored, sliced peppers along with the onions. Omit the peas.

variations

mixed-bean salad

see base recipe page 224

chickpea salad
Prepare the basic recipe, substituting 140 g (5 oz) cooked chickpeas for the mixed beans. If chickpeas are tinned, rinse and drain, and omit salt from recipe.

black bean & mango salad
Prepare the basic recipe, substituting 140 g (5 oz) cooked black beans and 140 g (5 oz) finely chopped mangoes for the mixed beans. If you use tinned black beans, rinse, drain and omit salt from recipe.

sweetcorn salad
Prepare the basic recipe, substituting 300 g (11 oz) thawed frozen sweetcorn for the mixed beans.

potato & pea salad
Prepare the basic recipe, substituting 140 g (5 oz) finely chopped boiled potatoes and 140 g (5 oz) thawed frozen peas for the mixed beans.

tuna salad
Prepare basic recipe, substituting 140 g (5 oz) tinned flaked tuna in water for the mixed beans. Rinse and drain the tuna before adding. Omit salt.

variations

sprout salad

see base recipe page 227

carrot salad
Prepare the basic recipe, substituting 225 g (8 oz) grated carrots for the sprouts.

beetroot salad
Prepare the basic recipe, substituting 280 g (10 oz) grated beetroot for the sprouts.

radish salad
Prepare the basic recipe, substituting 140 g (5 oz) thinly sliced radishes for the sprouts.

cabbage salad
Prepare the basic recipe, substituting 225 g (8 oz) finely sliced cabbage for the sprouts.

cucumber salad
Prepare the basic recipe, substituting 140 g (5 oz) finely chopped cucumber for the sprouts.

tomato salad
Prepare the basic recipe, substituting 360 g (13 oz) finely chopped tomatoes for the sprouts.

variations

spiced potato salad

see base recipe page 228

sweet potato salad
Prepare the basic recipe, substituting 340 g (12 oz) sliced sweet potatoes for the regular potatoes.

spiced beetroot salad
Prepare the basic recipe, substituting 280 g (10 oz) sliced beetroot for the potatoes.

spiced cauliflower salad
Prepare the basic recipe, substituting 140 g (5 oz) sliced cauliflower florets for the potatoes.

spiced carrot salad
Prepare the basic recipe, substituting 225 g (8 oz) sliced carrots for the potatoes.

variations

masala slaw

see base recipe page 230

creamy potato salad
Prepare the basic recipe, substituting 340 g (12 oz) finely chopped boiled potatoes for both types of cabbage.

creamy chickpea salad
Prepare the basic recipe, substituting 400 g (14 oz) cooked chickpeas for both types of cabbage. If chickpeas are tinned, rinse and drain before using and omit salt from recipe.

creamy cauliflower salad
Prepare the basic recipe, substituting 140 g (5 oz) finely chopped steamed cauliflower for both types of cabbage.

creamy broccoli & carrot slaw
Prepare the basic recipe, substituting 225 g (8 oz) shredded broccoli and carrots for both types of cabbage.

variations

chickpea & onion salad

see base recipe page 232

chickpea & potato salad
Prepare the basic recipe, substituting 2 medium potatoes, cut into
2.5-cm (1-in) cubes and deep-fried until crisp, for the onions.

chickpea & pea salad
Prepare the basic recipe, substituting 300 g (11 oz) thawed frozen peas for
the onions.

chickpea & sweetcorn salad
Prepare the basic recipe, substituting 300 g (11 oz) thawed frozen sweetcorn
for the onions.

variations

cumin rice

see base recipe page 233

fennel rice
Prepare the basic recipe, substituting 1 tablespoon fennel seeds for the cumin.

sesame rice
Prepare the basic recipe, substituting 1 tablespoon sesame seeds for the cumin.

mint rice
Prepare the basic recipe, adding in 1 tablespoon dried mint along with the rice.

saffron rice
Prepare the basic recipe, adding in 1 teaspoon saffron threads along with
the rice.

lemon rice
Prepare the basic recipe, adding in 1 tablespoon lemon zest along with the rice.

variations

coriander & mint rice

see base recipe page 235

coriander & lemon rice
Prepare the basic recipe, substituting 2 tablespoons lemon zest for the mint.

mint & lemon rice
Prepare the basic recipe, substituting 2 tablespoons lemon zest for the coriander.

coriander & dill rice
Prepare the basic recipe, substituting fresh dill for the mint.

variations

cranberry & raisin pulao

see base recipe page 236

cranberry & sweetcorn pulao

Prepare the basic recipe, substituting 140 g (5 oz) frozen sweetcorn for the raisins.

cranberry & plum pulao

Prepare the basic recipe, substituting 30 g (1 oz) chopped dried plums (prunes) for the raisins.

cranberry & almond pulao

Prepare the basic recipe, substituting 30 g (1 oz) blanched almonds for the raisins.

variations

tomato rice

see base recipe page 238

tomato rice with peas & carrots
Prepare the basic recipe, adding a total of 140 g (5 oz) frozen peas and carrots along with the tomatoes.

tomato rice with raisins
Prepare the basic recipe, adding 30 g (1 oz) raisins along with the tomatoes.

tomato rice with mushrooms
Prepare the basic recipe, adding 140 g (5 oz) chopped mushrooms along with the tomatoes.

variations

chicken pulao

see base recipe page 241

chicken pulao with peas
Prepare the basic recipe, adding 140 g (5 oz) frozen peas along with the rice.

chicken pulao with raisins
Prepare the basic recipe, adding 30 g (1 oz) raisins along with the chicken.

chicken pulao with plums
Prepare the basic recipe, adding 30 g (1 oz) chopped dried plums (prunes) along with the chicken.

variations

besan chila

see base recipe page 242

besan chila with tomatoes
Prepare the basic recipe, adding in 1 small finely chopped tomato into
the batter.

besan chila with mint
Prepare the basic recipe, substituting fresh mint leaves for the fresh
coriander leaves.

besan chila with dill
Prepare the basic recipe, substituting fresh dill for the fresh
coriander leaves.

besan chila with onions
Prepare the basic recipe, adding in 1 finely chopped onion into the batter.

besan chila with peas
Prepare the basic recipe, adding in 30 g (1 oz) thawed and mashed frozen green
peas into the batter.

besan chila with carrots
Prepare the basic recipe, adding in 30 g (1 oz) grated carrots into the batter.

variations

instant dosa

see base recipe page 244

courgette dosa

Prepare the basic recipe, substituting grated courgette for the carrots.

pea dosa

Prepare the basic recipe, substituting 85 g (3 oz) thawed frozen peas for the carrots.

sweetcorn dosa

Prepare the basic recipe, substituting 85 g (3 oz) thawed frozen sweetcorn for the carrots.

potato dosa

Prepare the basic recipe, substituting grated boiled potatoes for the carrots.

radish dosa

Prepare the basic recipe, substituting grated radishes for the carrots.

cabbage dosa

Prepare the basic recipe, substituting finely chopped cabbage for the carrots.

chutneys
& relishes

Indian cooking has the perfect chutney or relish

to go with any dish, from cooling raita to sweet

mango chutney. Use them as sides, dips or as a

spread on your everyday sandwiches.

kachumber

see variations page 274

Kachumber literally means cut into 'small pieces', and this dish is a side of finely chopped and refreshing vegetables. Pair it with some yoghurt, which in India is often served alongside curry to cut down on the heat level of the food, since the cool creaminess of the yoghurt helps lessen the spice impact on the palate.

140 g (5 oz) cucumber, finely chopped
140 g (5 oz) tomatoes, finely chopped
85 g (3 oz) onion, finely chopped
2 tbsp fresh coriander leaves, finely chopped
1 jalapeño pepper, including seeds,
　finely chopped

$\frac{1}{4}$ tsp red chilli powder
$\frac{1}{4}$ tsp garlic powder
$\frac{1}{4}$ tsp cumin powder
salt, to taste
1 tbsp olive oil
2 tbsp fresh lemon juice

Mix all the ingredients in a bowl and set the dish in the fridge for 15–20 minutes to allow all the flavours to blend. Before serving, give it a good mix again. This dish doesn't keep well, so it should be eaten the same day it is made.

Serves 4

onion & garlic relish

see variations page 275

Indian cuisine favours strong robust flavours, and there is no better way for them to come through than in a relish like this one.

2 tbsp light cooking oil
1 tsp cumin seeds
1 tsp mustard seeds
2 tbsp minced garlic

400 g (14 oz) thinly sliced onions
2 tbsp sugar
$\frac{1}{2}$ tsp red chilli powder
salt, to taste

Heat oil in a wide pan. Add in cumin and mustard seeds. Once they start to sizzle, add garlic and sauté for a few seconds.

Add onions and sugar, and sauté until onions start to soften and brown. Add chilli powder and salt, and fry for another 5 minutes. Take the pan off the heat and allow to cool before serving. The relish will keep in the fridge for about a week.

Serves 4

mint chutney

see variations page 276

Chutneys started out as a way to make use of leftover ingredients. In most cases, they are prepared fresh, to be consumed immediately.

140 g (5 oz) fresh mint leaves, chopped
85 g (3 oz) fresh coriander leaves, chopped
1–2 green chillies, including seeds, chopped

1–2 garlic cloves
salt, to taste
1 tbsp lemon juice

Mix all the ingredients in a bowl and let the chutney rest in the fridge for 15–20 minutes. Serve chilled.

Serves 4

mango chutney

see variations page 277

You can make a big batch of this chutney and store it in clean airtight glass jars in the fridge. It will stay fresh for about a week but it can also be frozen.

2 large ripe mangoes, peeled, seeded and
   chopped
140 g (5 oz) fresh mint leaves, chopped

$^{1}/_{2}$ tsp red chilli powder
1 tsp sugar
salt, to taste

Put all the ingredients in the blender and blend to form a smooth paste.

Serves 4

spiced tomato relish

see variations page 278

This chutney is a great accompaniment to stuffed Indian breads called parathas, and works perfectly served alongside a simple dal.

2 tbsp light cooking oil
1 tsp cumin seeds
1 tsp mustard seeds
7–8 fresh curry leaves
2–3 garlic cloves, sliced
1 medium onion, finely chopped

$\frac{1}{2}$ tsp red chilli powder
2 large tomatoes, finely chopped
salt, to taste
water, if needed
fresh coriander leaves, finely chopped,
    for garnish

Heat oil in a frying pan or saucepan and sauté cumin seeds, mustard seeds and curry leaves until they start to sizzle. Add in garlic and sauté for a few seconds. Add in onions and fry until they start to soften and lightly brown.

Add in chilli powder, tomatoes and salt, and cook on a low heat for 15–20 minutes until the tomatoes pulp and blend well with the onions. Add in a little bit of water if the tomatoes start to dry up and stick to the pan.

Garnish with fresh coriander leaves. Will keep in the fridge for 3 days.

Serves 4

sweet tamarind chutney

see variations page 279

The tamarind is a tropical Asian tree that has edible fruit. Tamarind chutney, made from that fruit, is a classic Indian dip. It varies in taste, depending on the region that it comes from. The southern part of India tends to make it more sweet than sour; northern India prefers its chutneys to be more tart.

140 g (5 oz) tamarind paste
500 ml (17 fl oz) water
140 g (5 oz) jaggery (brown sugar
    can be used as a substitute)

$1/2$ tsp red chilli powder
$1/4$ tsp dried ginger powder
salt, to taste

Put tamarind paste, water and jaggery in a deep pan and bring to the boil.

Add red chilli powder, ginger powder and salt, and continue to boil over a medium heat until the sauce starts to thicken and coats the back of a spoon.

Allow to cool and store in an airtight container in the fridge. Will keep for one week.

Serves 4

raita

see variations page 280

This version of raita is a simple homemade Indian recipe. In most Indian homes, a raita is made with a variety of vegetables or spices. Cucumbers add a subtle sweetness to the natural yoghurt and give it a wonderful texture.

260 g (9 oz) natural yoghurt, full fat or low fat
140 g (5 oz) grated cucumber
pinch of red chilli powder

pinch of garam masala
2 tbsp fresh mint leaves, finely chopped
salt, to taste

Mix all the ingredients to blend well. Set aside in the fridge so the raita is cool before serving. Use the same day, as raita doesn't store well.

Serves 4

garlic–yoghurt dip

see variations page 281

Yoghurt-based dips don't keep well and will lose their fresh flavour quickly. Use within a few hours of preparation.

140 g (5 oz) thick yoghurt, like Greek yoghurt
1 garlic clove, grated
pinch of red chilli powder
pinch of cumin powder

pinch of dried mint
salt, to taste
1 tbsp fresh lemon juice

Mix all the ingredients to blend well. Serve cold.

Serves 2

variations

kachumber

see base recipe page 259

kachumber with mint
Prepare the basic recipe, adding 1 tablespoon dried mint along with the spices.

kachumber with dill
Prepare the basic recipe, adding 2 tablespoons chopped dill along with the spices. Omit the coriander leaves.

kachumber with lemon
Prepare the basic recipe, adding 1 tablespoon lemon zest along with the spices.

kachumber with fennel
Prepare the basic recipe, adding 1 tablespoon crushed fennel seeds along with the spices.

kachumber with black pepper
Prepare the basic recipe, adding 1 tablespoon crushed black peppercorns along with the spices.

variations

onion & garlic relish

see base recipe page 260

onion relish flatbread

Prepare the basic recipe. Spread a thin layer of the relish on a plain naan and bake in an oven preheated to 175°C/Gas Mark 4 (350°F) for 8–10 minutes until the naan begins to crisp. Cut into slices and serve warm.

onion relish mashed potatoes

Prepare the basic recipe. Boil and mash 3 large potatoes and mix in the relish to blend well to make this tasty side dish.

mint chutney

see base recipe page 263

coriander chutney

Prepare the basic recipe, omitting the mint and increasing the fresh coriander leaves to 260 g (9 oz).

mint & tomato chutney

Prepare the basic recipe, adding 1 small tomato along with the rest of the ingredients.

coriander & tomato chutney

Prepare the basic recipe, omitting the mint and increasing the fresh coriander to 260 g (9 oz). Then add 1 small tomato with the rest of the ingredients.

variations

mango chutney

see base recipe page 264

pineapple chutney
Prepare the basic recipe, substituting 260 g (9 oz) chopped pineapple for the mangoes.

peach chutney
Prepare the basic recipe, substituting 300 g (11 oz) chopped peaches for the mangoes.

apricot chutney
Prepare the basic recipe, substituting 300 g (11 oz) chopped apricots for the mangoes.

variations

spiced tomato relish

see base recipe page 266

tomato relish flatbread
Prepare the basic recipe. Spread a thin layer of the relish on a plain naan and bake in an oven preheated to 175°C/Gas Mark 4 (350°F) for 8–10 minutes until the naan begins to crisp. Cut into slices and serve warm.

tomato relish mashed potatoes
Prepare the basic recipe. Boil and mash 3 large potatoes and mix in the relish to blend well for a tasty side dish.

tomato relish mashed cauliflower
Prepare the basic recipe. Boil and mash one medium-sized cauliflower and mix in to blend well for a tasty side dish.

variations

sweet tamarind chutney

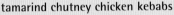see base recipe page 269

tamarind chutney chicken kebabs

Prepare the basic recipe. Marinate 2 chicken breasts, cut up into 2.5-cm (1-in)
pieces, in the chutney for at least 30 minutes. Place chicken pieces on a
preheated, oiled griddle and cook on the hob until done, turning chicken to
brown on each side.

tamarind chutney paneer kebabs

Prepare the basic recipe. Marinate 450 g (1 lb) of paneer, cut up into 2.5-cm
(1-in) pieces, in the chutney for at least 30 minutes. Place paneer pieces on a
preheated, oiled griddle and cook on the hob until done, turning paneer to
brown each side.

tamarind chutney prawns kebabs

Prepare the basic recipe. Marinate 900 g (2 lbs) of peeled and deveined prawns
in the chutney for at least 30 minutes. Place prawns on a preheated, oiled
griddle and cook on the hob until done, turning prawns to brown both sides.

variations

raita

see base recipe page 270

beetroot raita
Prepare the basic recipe, substituting 140 g (5 oz) beetroot for the cucumber.

potato raita
Prepare the basic recipe, substituting 140 g (5 oz) boiled grated potato for the cucumber.

carrot raita
Prepare the basic recipe, substituting 140 g (5 oz) carrots for the cucumber.

courgette raita
Prepare the basic recipe, substituting 140 g (5 oz) courgette for the cucumber.

mango raita
Prepare the basic recipe, substituting 140 g (5 oz) finely chopped mangoes for the cucumber.

variations

garlic–yoghurt dip

see base recipe page 273

garlic–yoghurt dip with coriander
Prepare the basic recipe, substituting 2 tablespoons fresh coriander leaves for the dried mint.

garlic–yoghurt dip with dill
Prepare the basic recipe, substituting 2 tablespoons minced fresh dill for the dried mint.

garlic–yoghurt dip with fennel
Prepare the basic recipe, substituting 1 teaspoon crushed fennel seeds for the dried mint.

index